WHAT'S YOUR NEXT MOVE?

E very day, we move in one direction or another. We're free to choose from endless possibilities. Only *you* can choose the direction for the rest of your life. Whether you are a seasoned executive, emerging leader, stay-at-home parent, or college student, frustration is inevitable. Now is the time for you to *SHIFT* from, "I'm so busy and stressed," to, "I'm living my ideal life right now." And it doesn't even have to be complicated.

In *SHIFT*, author Derek Deprey teaches you a 5-gear process. Each gear uniquely moves you from frustrated to fulfilled. Within each interactive chapter, you'll drive up to powerful questions and practical exercises—calls to make today the day you are inspired to change.

Through captivating storytelling and compelling exercises, you'll discover how to

- Confront your fears
- Form your core values
- Pursue personal growth
- Visualize your preferred future
- Adopt a positive mindset
- Personalize your ambitions
- Exercise meaningful action
- Fulfill your ideal life
- Inspire fellow travelers

Now is the time to reach your true potential. The right move, at the right moment, can make all the difference. If something stands between you and your ideal life, *SHIFT*. If you're looking for someone to help you maneuver the challenging territory, Derek is your fellow traveler as you point your compass in the right direction.

DEREK DEPREY's passion in life is to evoke excellence in every person at every level. After a career of working in basketball operations at the collegiate and professional levels, he empowers others both as a general manager at a fitness club and as a leadership professor at a university. Derek founded Move Results to impact the lives of individuals, organizations, and communities. Today, he loves to inspire and influence others as a speaker, writer, and coach. Derek lives in Milwaukee, WI, with his wife and two daughters.

Connect at DerekDeprey.com

PRAISE FOR *SHIFT*

"Just like our business at Northwestern Mutual is about helping people build brighter futures, Derek's goal in *SHIFT* is to help you make every decision with an eye toward your vision." **John Schlifske, chief executive officer at Northwestern Mutual**

"Derek's chapter on passions would single-handedly justify the book. Work doesn't have to be boring. Read *SHIFT* and you'll find your reason to wake up in the morning." **George Karl, 2013 NBA Coach of the Year, fifth most career wins in NBA history, and author of *Furious George***

"*SHIFT* will help you be more present, live your potential, and become the best version of yourself. Derek will help you overcome your frustrations and create your own definition of success that will reshape how you think about yourself." **Shawn Achor, Author of *The New York Times* bestsellers *Before Happiness* and *The Happiness Advantage***

"Derek's real message is that anyone can cultivate fulfillment through the masterfully integrated metaphor of a 5-speed manual car shifter. Within each gear, Derek weaves personal stories, examples, and suggestions with tangible action exercises." **Kary Oberbrunner, author of *ELIXIR Project, Day Job to Dream Job, The Deeper Path,* and *Your Secret Name***

"*SHIFT* is a must-read book for all job seekers to help them determine their attitude, discover their passions, and design their execution. Derek's proven path gives you the tips, tools, and tactics that you need to get in gear and back on track." **Wayne Breitbarth, author of** *The Power Formula for LinkedIn Success: Kick-Start Your Business, Brand, and Job Search*

"Ever since the first time I met Derek, he has been full of energy for helping people get better. That is one reason that we rushed to hire him at Marquette. I am not surprised he is continuing his passion of helping people in *SHIFT*. Derek is proof of how much you can grow as a person and in life once you decide to face your deepest frustrations and fears. He is providing a game plan for people to turn their have-tos into their want-tos." **Tom Crean, head coach at Indiana University men's basketball**

"Derek provides just the right balance of thinking and doing. *SHIFT* is packed with thought-provoking questions and hands-on activities that will get you moving right away." **Keith Nygren, founder and president at the Wisconsin Athletic Club**

"Much like my book *Moving the Needle*, *SHIFT* is a roadmap that will help you move the needle in your personal and professional life. Derek understands, teaches, and lives the concepts and helps others daily." **Joe Sweeney, author of** *Moving the Needle* **and** *The New York Times* **best seller** *Networking is a Contact Sport*

"From the moment I met Derek, I have been consistently impressed with his intelligence, energy, and passion for growth. *SHIFT* puts all three in your hands, along with a roadmap to your happiest future. With Derek's practical advice, all the things you wondered about become possible. *SHIFT* now!" **Susan Marshall, author of** *How to Grow a Backbone: 10 Strategies for Gaining Power and Influence at Work*

"What an inspiring, well-written book! There are many people every day that would love to *SHIFT* their current life situation from frustrated to fulfilled. This book is a roadmap to making that a reality." **Larry Harris, assistant GM and director of player personnel of the Golden State Warriors and former GM of the Milwaukee Bucks**

"Derek teaches you that personal growth can be rewarding and enjoyable as you maximize God-given strengths within a strategic process. Follow the cues that get you excited. *SHIFT* is a remarkable book." **Dr. Daniel Johnson, president at Wisconsin Lutheran College, *U.S. News & World Report* Top 20 Midwest College**

"*SHIFT* has been able to help me think about work from a different perspective. I stopped striving for work–life balance and started living work–life fusion. Derek's personal stories are so relatable that you'll never forget what you're learning." **Syneathia LaGrant, vice president of Global People Development at Molson Coors**

"Derek is simply a wise coach for your mind and your body. *SHIFT* is a must read to 'tune up' your future physically, mentally, and spiritually." **Jim Mizes, president at Blaze Pizza**

"If Derek writes it, I read it. I do not know of a leader who is more intentional about investing in people than he is. Derek understands the difference between genuine character and superficial reputation. He has experienced the satisfaction and frustration of competitive athletics along with the challenges the real world provides every day. Simply put, his insight is not based on ivory tower speculation. His wisdom is grounded in the lessons learned from victory and defeat. *SHIFT* will help keep you focused and moving forward." **Jack Bennett, former University of Wisconsin-Stevens Point Head basketball coach, National Coach of the Year, and back-to-back NCAA Division III champion**

"His practical advice combined with templates and process will allow you to take the huge task of designing your life around what matters and creating implementable steps in every aspect of your personal and professional life. Read *SHIFT* if you want to stop saying, 'I'm so busy,' or, 'I'm so stressed,' and you want to start living the life you were born to live. As an attention expert, I believe in paying attention to what matters and making the most of creating significant moments. Derek's book will help you do that. Buy it for your team and your loved ones." **Neen James, author of *Attention Pays: Creating Moments that Matter* and *Folding Time: How to Achieve Twice as Much in Half the Time* "**

"*SHIFT* is not just any book. I feel like I am attending a live workshop vs. reading a book. It is both relevant and inspiring. Derek's encouraging approach is right up my alley." **Bill Mcbride, cofounder, president and CEO of Active Wellness and BMC3, and former chairman of the board of directors, IHRSA**

"If you've been wondering where to go on life's journey, *SHIFT* is your easy-to-follow personal navigation system. Derek helps you choose a destination, steer clear of wrong turns, and reflect when you run into obstacles and dead ends." **Virginia Pothier, author of *The Happiness Journey* and CEO and founder of Hapacus**

"*SHIFT* made me a better wife, mom, friend, and colleague. An inspiring, refreshing, and page-turning read, Derek's 5-gear process was easy to digest and implement." **Stacy Tuschl, Author of #1 International best seller *Is Your Business Worth Saving?***

SHIFT

SHIFT

MOVE FROM
FRUSTRATED TO FULFILLED

DEREK DEPREY

AUTHOR elite
ACADEMY

Printed in the United States of America

Published by Author Academy Elite
P.O. Box 43, Powell, OH 43035

AuthorAcademyElite.com

Paperback ISBN-978-1-946114-03-7

Hardcover ISBN-978-1-946114-04-4

Library of Congress Control Number: 2016960987

I'm dedicating this book to my rock, my wife Rachel, and to our girls, Ellie and Mia.

I'm grateful that Rachel has joined me on our journey of personal growth and that she shares the burning desire to move us and our daughters to be the very best.

CONTENTS

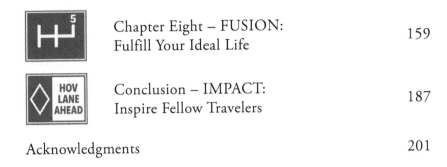

FOREWORD

Some people are frustrated. Some people are fulfilled. In *SHIFT*, it's clear my friend Derek Deprey knows the difference between the two. This book is significant to me because I value the development of true potential. In my book, *Day Job to Dream Job*, I, too, challenge you to experience fulfillment. What a delight it is to know that Derek and I are on similar paths in our lives.

Derek didn't start moving, growing, and impacting others until he noticed that what he was hiding from others was exactly what they wanted to see. You'll see in the pages that follow the proof of Derek's own journey of shifting gears from frustrated to fulfilled. Instead of just telling us, he shows us through a masterfully integrated metaphor of a 5-speed manual car shifter. Within each gear, Derek weaves personal stories, examples, and suggestions with tangible action exercises.

Consume *SHIFT* and you'll be able to move the stress and busyness that's standing between you and your ideal life. You'll learn how to confront your deepest frustrations, form your personal core values, pursue personal growth, visualize your preferred future, adopt a positive mindset, personalize your ambitions, exercise meaningful action, fulfill your ideal life, and inspire fellow travelers. Your career will grow, and your life will be more enjoyable.

As you read *SHIFT*, you'll probably have the same reaction as I did. "This seems so easy." The problem is that both Derek and I continue to see far too many frustrated people. What excites me is that there is a better way…a way to transform your life. I cannot think of a timelier solution. I'm grateful for Derek's willingness to be our driver through this important movement. *SHIFT* will be a roadmap for me for years to come. Be a learner, *SHIFT* through the gears, and you'll see how fulfillment is within your reach.

Kary Oberbrunner
CEO of Redeem the Day and Igniting Souls,
author of *ELIXIR Project*, *Day Job to Dream Job*,
The Deeper Path, and *Your Secret Name*

PREFACE

"Move confidently in the direction of your dreams.
Live the life you imagined."
– Henry David Thoreau

A re you stuck and seeking the next step to move forward? If you're looking for someone to help you maneuver the challenging territory, and to then help you celebrate your success...I'm your fellow traveler. I wrote this book to help you achieve your highest potential. I want to inspire you to live and to love your most ideal life, starting today. Now is the time to choose the direction you want your life to take. It's time for you to zealously make the necessary moves—in your life, your career, and in your home—that will take you in that direction.

Do you feel like you're striving to do the best you can, struggling hard to meet the demands that come at you? Are you scrambling to figure out where you'd even begin to transform your life and pursue your dreams? Moving toward your most fulfilling life will be a never-ending journey. While some of us may be headed in the same direction, each of us will experience a very different path. We were all created for a distinctive purpose, and each of us offers something to the world that is uniquely personal. I am constantly learning about what I value, what I love, and what I am good at. Knowing who I am gives me the foundation that allows me to forever be moving closer to living out my purpose and passion.

Every day, I'm filled with enthusiasm for what lies ahead. Today, there is an ease to my work and my life, but that wasn't always the case. Identifying your values and vision will set a firm foundation and preferred future for your journey.

Could one move change your life? Every day, we move in one direction or another. We're free to choose from endless opportunities and possibilities. Personal growth and development are vital factors in staying on course and making steady progress. I created my own business, Move Results, because of the deep commitment I have to personal growth and because I believe the best business to start is the one that you need yourself. I have developed a principle and process that has resulted in practical, meaningful, and sustained growth. I've learned how to execute my passions with a positive attitude, and it has changed my life. I teach and inspire others to do the same, so that they can grow and live from the truest, most genuine parts of themselves. In both my personal and professional lives, I have the privilege of connecting with many amazing people. I often hear them say that they don't know how to grow, and they ask me if I can teach them how to do just that. Exploring and developing your attitudes, passions, and actions is the formula for expanding your personal growth.

Along our journey, we'll face many different situations. Each of these situations is unique for each of us. We'll achieve desired outcomes, we'll experience being in the zone, and eventually we'll find our sweet spot. While reading *SHIFT* may seem like only a small move in the right direction, it just might end up being the most significant move that you make in your life. You just have to get started.

Every success, no matter how big or small, is evidence of growth and movement. Once we start our journey, we will also encounter difficulties. We won't always achieve what we set out to do, and we may get confused and feel lost. Thankfully, our failures will also result in growth and movement if we're willing to learn from our mistakes. Just like you, I've experienced both success and failure. I've crashed and I've overcome obstacles. I do my best to meet whatever comes my way with a positive attitude, confidence, and an eagerness to learn the lessons along the way. Regardless of the conditions we face, we don't have to journey alone. We're here to learn and grow together. I'm on your team. I'll help you.

Only *you* can choose the direction of the rest of your life. You know that you're absolutely capable of transforming your life and moving closer to living your dreams. You've always had what it takes to make the first move, and you always will. Turn the key—today you will choose to start your new life. We will move toward your ideal life…together!

INTRODUCTION

CRASH:
CONFRONT YOUR
DEEPEST FRUSTRATIONS

*"I've come to believe that all my past failures
and frustrations were actually laying the foundation
for the understandings that have created
the new level of living I now enjoy."*

– Tony Robbins

I 'll never forget it. It was the spring of 2006. I was the coordinator of basketball operations for the Marquette University men's
basketball team. We were coming off a solid season and had made
it to the esteemed NCAA Basketball Tournament. About one month
after our last game, we had our annual post-season banquet to celebrate
our season.

On the day of the banquet, I arrived at our practice facility
early in the morning to work on our summer basketball camps.
When head coach Tom Crean walked into the building, he asked
me to present the Hit the Deck award to one of our players. It was
basically a toughness award for physical play, for someone who
consistently sacrificed his body for the team.

I had ten hours to figure out what to say, and I was sweating about it throughout the day. I was so terrified of getting up in front of the crowd. I could feel my anxiety building up minute by minute, getting worse and worse as the day progressed. I was a nervous wreck. At lunch, after everyone left the office, I decided to check out the VHS archives for the Hit the Deck award banquet speeches from the previous two years. I wrote down and studied what the other coaches said. I decided to basically memorize what one coach had said, naively thinking I had it all figured out and everything was going to be fine.

The Crash: My Deepest Frustration

It was 6:00 p.m. when the Marquette fans started arriving. The crowd was filled with some amazing people, like NBA All-Star Dwyane Wade, who was giving autographs all night; ESPN college basketball analyst Digger Phelps, who gave the keynote address; and a number of highly successful millionaires who had donated to the basketball program.

At 7:52 p.m. sharp, my name was announced. Blinded by the spotlight, I walked up to the podium and said, "Tonight, I'm honored to present the Hit the Deck award winner." As I caught sight of the staring faces, I immediately froze. I completely went blank. Everything I had memorized suddenly flew out the window. Here I was, paralyzed with fear in front of the crowd of people. I even looked down and shook my head in disgust. All I could remember to say was, "And the award goes to Joe Chapman."

Because I failed to give Joe his praise, Coach Crean came back up to the stage to give Joe the words that he deserved. Coach Crean said, "Joe laid it all out on the line every day. He became an outstanding leader for this team by example and through his toughness. Joe had people write him off, but he came back and competed at such a high level."

When I walked back to my table, my colleagues were quiet and had deer-in-the-headlights looks on their faces. They'd quickly glance at me and then look away. I wanted to crawl into a hole and never see any of them again. I was so embarrassed and humiliated by what had happened. I was the perfectionist who bombed.

Does my story help you relate to a time in your life when you crashed?

The Stall

After deeply reflecting on this dreadful memory, I realized this moment wasn't just a random epic failure. It was, in fact, a buildup of events that had haunted me over the years. I had been stalling and trying to avoid doing anything in front of groups since I was seven (with the exception of playing basketball). It was my obstacle for growth.

In second grade, our teacher gave us the assignment to read a book and then do an oral report in front of the class. I selected *The Tortoise and the Hare*. When the day arrived for my speech, I stood in front of the class, froze, didn't say a word, and walked back to my desk broken.

In fifth grade, our teacher wanted us to sing the scale in front of the class. I sang, "Do-Re-Mi." I cried, "Fa-So-La-Ti-Do." A few of my classmates have never let me forget that breakdown.

In my sophomore speech class, the minimum expectation was to give a five-minute speech about anything we wanted. Mine lasted fifty-eight seconds. By then, I had almost learned to expect that I would fail.

As a high school senior on the basketball team, I let my co-captain Brent Hansen lead all our huddles with motivational words. I stood there wanting to say something so badly, but I never did.

As a college senior on our basketball team, I feared that our coach would call on me to lead the pregame prayer in front of the team. When he did, I shared the shortest prayer in history. "Dear Lord, thank you for giving us the opportunity to play this great game. Amen."

As the director of the Marquette University men's basketball camp, I avoided speaking in front of the camp coaches. Instead, I let the assistant camp director Kevin McKenna lead while I stood in the back of the room with a clipboard and acted busy.

So it's really no wonder why the crash at the men's basketball banquet happened about twenty years after my second grade book report. I'd never confronted my biggest fear of speaking in front of others. Instead, I dreaded going into work for each of the next 365 days. I'd beat myself up over my freezing up every time I'd see someone who was at the banquet, which was over five times per day. I didn't want to face my peers. I didn't want to face the players. I had an early midlife crisis. It didn't matter how much money or status I had because the crash left me empty on the inside.

I did, however, decide that it was time to face my fear. I knew this dreadful memory would haunt me for a very long time. Even though this was a traumatic experience, it taught me lessons so valuable that they're hard to put into words. The crash gifted me with an intense drive to always strive to be better. It also showed me that like Joe, I'd have to be tough enough to move on. However, I'd need another nudge, and I would get just that.

The Brutally Honest Feedback

After the crash, I stayed at Marquette University for one more season. During my second year at Marquette, Coach Crean said something to me in the video room that would change my life forever. He said to me, **"If your confidence doesn't start matching your quality of work, you'll never be a head coach."** I realized that he was telling me that my work output behind the scenes was awesome, but my confidence with people and in front of people was shaky. Did I want to hear this from one of the most respected head coaches in the country? No. Was it exactly what I needed to hear? No doubt.

Time to Move On

Unfortunately, I clammed up even more. Not being able to overcome my fear was nobody's fault but my own. During the 2006–2007 basketball season at Marquette, I realized that to overcome the crash, I would have to leave the school. To begin my new journey, I had to start elsewhere with a renewed sense of confidence. Thankfully, my mentor Jim Boylen was appointed the head coach for the University of Utah men's basketball team. A few weeks later, Coach Boylen hired me as the director of player development, and my wife Rachel and I moved to Utah.

While at Utah, nobody knew my history of public speaking. I started to overcome my fear of speaking to some degree. As soon as I arrived, I dove in headfirst and led our basketball camps looking down at my heavy notes so I wouldn't crash. I tried really hard to have my confidence in front of other people match the quality of my work behind the scenes.

Why Did I Crash?

I often ask myself, "Why did the stall and finally the crash really happen?" I mean, people would tell me that I had it all. I had a loving family. I had my faith. I was healthy and was a good athlete. I was a decent student and had been the prom king. I even had some financial success. The reality is that I didn't "have it all." I fought the demon of speaking in front of others every day.

So, why did I crash? I definitely agree that I lacked the confidence that Coach Crean had pointed out to me. But why did I lack that confidence? This was the key. I didn't know how to grow. I was not introduced to personal growth and development until 2008. Growth and development from my own personal crash drives me each and every day to become a better speaker. Realizing the why of a failure is necessary for growth.

🛑 Your Crash

What do you feel frustrated about? Is that the place to start on your journey to fulfillment? Think about some of your failures and deep frustrations in your life. Jot some of them down. You must be brutally honest with your frustrations if you want to be fulfilled.

_____

_____

_____

_____

_____

Looking at your list of failures, circle the one that is holding you back from living your ideal day right now. This is your crash. Mine was the big public speaking fail at Marquette. But don't let twenty years go by between your crash and success. Why is your crash so important for you to reveal and confront? My mentor and coach, Kary Oberbrunner, said it best. **"The area of your biggest wound is often the area of your biggest contribution."** Chances are, a crash is what's holding you back from considering yourself successful.

But Wait. What Is Success?

You're closer to success than you think. But what is success? According to Google, there are about 1.2 billion links about success. Over 1 billon links should make anyone realize that success isn't a one-size-fits-all model for everyone. Stop looking to others for what success is and isn't.

For the purposes of defining and achieving success, it's crucial to note that you are running your own race, not anyone else's race. You'll learn that you cannot compare your success to others. Don't let someone else define success for you. Instead, make sure to compare yourself yesterday to yourself today. My friend Mike Kinsella reminds me, "You're either getting better or you're getting worse…there is no such thing as staying the same." Once you can successfully do that, you'll be on the right path. What does success mean to you?

According to leadership guru John Maxwell, "Success means having those closest to me love and respect me the most." Author and speaker Darren Hardy will tell you, "Success is personal growth." Legendary NCAA basketball coach John Wooden taught, "Success is peace of mind, which is a direct result of self-satisfaction in knowing you made the effort to do your best to become the best that you are capable of becoming."

🛑 Your Definition of Success

Reflect on and write down your definition of success.

_____

_____

_____

_____

_____

There is no wrong answer when defining what success means to you as an individual. Only you know what results you want to achieve. I define success as "living your ideal day right now."

> I define success as "living your ideal day right now."

Are you living your ideal day right now?

Think about your ideal day…a day that is perfect in your mind. By ideal day, I don't mean taking a day of vacation and sitting on the beach for sixteen hours and sleeping for the other eight. I'm talking about what your normal day—the day that you might be trying to escape from—would ideally look like to you. During your ideal day, you might be baking, listening to music, taking a walk with your spouse, working at your dream job, reading a book with a cup of coffee, volunteering, exercising with a friend, playing with your children, or meditating.

🛑 Your Ideal Day

Take a moment right now to dream about your ideal day. What are you doing that ignites your soul? Why are you doing it? Who are you with? Where are you? When are you doing it? How are you feeling?

_____

_____

_____

_____

_____

As you *SHIFT* and start to move through the gears, your ideal day will become clearer…and you'll learn how to make your ideal day become your real day!

Now Is the Time to Get in Gear

I don't know where you are right now while you're reading this book. You may be in a coffee shop, in bed, at the gym, or at a bookstore. Wherever you are physically, I want you to stop and think about your potential mentally. My goal is for you to mark up this book and move closer to your God-given potential. You, and only you, have the ability to make a difference for yourself, your family, and your organization. You are 100 percent responsible. Age is not a factor. It's never too late to change your life, as you can live your life fulfilled regardless of age. Think about the ideal day that you just noted. How often do you live your ideal day? After reading this book, you'll know better how to make living your ideal day a reality.

Frustrated or Fulfilled: Where Are You Headed?

This book is organized into five gears. Each one uniquely shifts you from frustrated to fulfilled. You'll feel frustrated when you experience distress and annoyance, especially because of the inability to change or to achieve something. On the other hand, you'll find yourself satisfied or happy when you've fully developed your abilities or character. Together, we'll stop saying, "Oh, shoot!" as we drive away from frustration, and happily proclaim, "Just *SHIFT!*" as we proceed toward fulfillment.

Be a Learner. We're All Growing.

I'll share my successes and failures with high energy, endless passion, and positive, unshakable confidence accompanying each of my endeavors. You just have to want to better yourself, to grow, and to live a joyful and fulfilled life. Like you, I'm still growing each day. We all are.

There is no perfect human being, although we all strive hard to become the best people we can be. This book is really all about the simple things in my life: stories about my experiences, challenges I've faced, things I've learned, obstacles I've overcome, my passions, and much more. But according to the legendary Jim Rohn, **"What's easy to do is also easy not to do."** Stay focused and be a learner.

I'm passionate about personal growth, and it's my sincere hope that my insatiable passion will be reflected through each of these chapters. Within each compelling chapter, there are powerful questions and a call to action...a call to make today the day you are inspired to change...not just for a week or a month, but for the rest of your life! When you see a STOP sign, pause from your reading and immediately get to work. These action exercises empower you to go from "know how" to "move now." If you don't strive for success today, a successful tomorrow never comes, and you're left with a life of regret and sorrow. Don't let that be you. Potential is meaningless without action.

Work through this book at your own pace. Don't just add *SHIFT* to your bookshelf. Take notes as you go. If you would prefer to write in a workbook, please visit **DerekDeprey.com/ShiftBookResources** for the complimentary download. Really take the time to think and reflect. When going through the questions, notice that these are not competitive questions, such as, "How many social media followers do you have," or, "How many boards are you on?" These are questions to help you become more mindful about what success and happiness means to you. You get what you put in. If you want to truly move from frustrated to fulfilled, then you must finish the book. If you get stuck, I'm here to help. Join my Shifting Gears Team private experience, and I'll coach you through the journey. For more information, please visit **DerekDeprey.com/ShiftingGearsTeam**

> There are opportunities everywhere…if you start to move.

There are opportunities everywhere…if you start to move. If now is the time to live your ideal day, then now is the time to grow. Let's look out the windshield, and begin to create a life that you love, not one that you merely settle on. I challenge you to *SHIFT* into drive right now. *SHIFT* leads to movement. Movement leads to growth.

> *SHIFT* leads to movement. Movement leads to growth.

Is Your Foundation Broken or Rock Solid?

To be able to move forward in life, you'll need great footing. In Gear One, you'll learn that the best way to create a solid foundation is to determine your true personal values. In the next chapter, I'll help you discover them. Once you do this, you'll be able to move forward purposefully, based on your rock-solid foundation of values. Your values are the ideas and virtues that are most important to you. Your values are the things that you won't compromise on, or that you would die to defend. When you consistently keep your personal values at the heart of everything you do, you'll create a smoother journey toward living your ideal life right now.

"Crash" Key Moves

- Discover the crash that is holding you back.
- Create your own definition of success.
- Start to build your ideal day around your definition of success.

To receive a one-page summary of *SHIFT*, please visit **DerekDeprey.com/ShiftBookResources** for your complimentary download.

STOP Write down the *first thing* from this chapter's content that you will move to act on.

_____

_____

_____

_____

_____

SHIFT Roadmap: From Crash to Foundation

CHAPTER ONE

FOUNDATION:
FORM YOUR CORE VALUES

*"It's not hard to make decisions once
you know what your values are."*

– Roy E. Disney

In 2003, as a twenty-three-year-old young buck (no pun intended), I was offered a position as an assistant video scout with the Milwaukee Bucks in the National Basketball Association (NBA). In other words, I was offered the lowest position on the totem pole on the basketball operations side of the business. I was stoked by the prospect of working for my favorite basketball team of all time, but there was one major drawback—the salary. The compensation for the job was just under $20,000. At that time, I was working as a sales representative somewhere else making nearly $40,000 annually. Naturally, I spoke with my parents and friends. Rather than telling me what I should do, my parents asked me an important question: "Money aside, which option would give you the most experience in the area that you ultimately want to work in for the long run?"

I immediately thought of the book *Oh, the Places You'll Go!* by Dr. Seuss, which my mom had gifted me for my college graduation, and the quote inside: "You have brains in your head. Your feet in your shoes. You can steer yourself in any direction you choose." My parents, in essence, were saying, "You don't have to do what we did." This is not a new concept. In fact, philosopher Soren Kierkegaard in the 1800s said that **you are individually responsible for giving meaning to life, living it with passion and authenticity, and taking a leap of faith to be *you*.** My parents have always supported me without judgment.

A Cracked Foundation

At the time, I didn't realize how significant my parents' question would become. Now I do. Their question exposed a crack in my foundation that was starting to get bigger and bigger. It was the first time that I was aware of the value conflict between money and passion. For the sake of this book, values will be defined as "what really matters to you." I realized that I was valuing money over passion, but I wasn't feeling successful. I wasn't living my ideal day or life. While most people would've scoffed at the idea of making just under $20,000 a year—less than their current salary—I did the exact opposite. After all, the opportunity to work for the Bucks could be a once-in-a-lifetime chance, and I knew that I needed to carefully weigh the pros and cons of each option.

It's this time in my life that reminds me of my personal core values and the foundation of growth. This is only one example of many in the arena of value conflict. Before the offer to work with the Bucks, I valued compensation over following my dream. I am forever grateful that my parents presented me with the question they did; otherwise, there's a good chance I would've let the financial gain take over and convince me to reject the position strictly because of the compensation. That would have been a huge mistake—one I would have regretted for years to come. My parents played a big part in providing the support I needed to seal the crack in my foundation. I ended up accepting the position, and I couldn't have been happier with my decision to pursue my dreams. This early experience was key to my future progress.

Why Are Core Values Important to Living Your Ideal Day?

Before we get too far, let me ask you this: why are values so important to living your ideal day? While there might be hundreds of reasons, let's focus on the biggest two: to guide your decision-making and to drive your actions.

Values help guide decision-making. As I mentioned, I valued my passion for a career that I loved over my desire to make more money. At that moment, I couldn't have both. The passion question from my parents steered my decision in the right direction, as it took my values into consideration.

Let me share another example that occurred during a job interview. I was the interviewee. The interviewer said that if they hired me, I'd have to remove the following words from my voicemail message because they weren't "corporate" enough: "I'm either making a difference in people's lives, or I'm spending time with my family." I knew that wasn't going to happen, because if I had made that tradeoff, I wouldn't have been able to be myself or live my values.

You see, values can help you start on your journey to fulfillment, and they'll end up defining you over time. You cannot have a real foundation without them…and you'll have nothing on which to base decisions and action. Values help to drive action and execution. My passion at the time to one day become a head basketball coach compelled me to take the necessary action of accepting the job with the Milwaukee Bucks for less money.

Core values are your guiding principles that dictate behavior and action. You won't feel rock solid until you know what's important to you.

> Core values are your guiding principles that dictate behavior and action.

Revealing My Core Values

I have a confession to make to you as well as to all my past teachers: in the year 2008, at age twenty-eight, I read a book in its entirety for the first time. The good news is that this gift, *The 21 Irrefutable*

Laws of Leadership by John C. Maxwell, quickly hooked me on self-improvement. What can you do that you've never done before...that you just might end up doing for the rest of your life?

During my early years of learning to grow, I read countless books and articles. I attended seminars across the country. I got involved in online communities and forums, and I talked to other experts in the industry to gain more knowledge and insight.

When juxtaposing the various success formulas to compare and contrast their core principles for success, I began noticing the different variables between them. Some of them were simple; others were quite complex and therefore difficult for some people to understand.

However, all the research from other gurus in the field has led to me to discover one major aha—the formulas for success narrow down to just a few simple but fundamental concepts. With this realization, I got to work and began to use my own personal values—which include attitude, passions, and execution—to develop my groundwork. Without values, there is no growth, no ideal day, and no ideal life.

Accepting the assistant video scout job with the Bucks turned out to be an amazing opportunity. I decided to take the job despite the low salary because my dream job at that time was to one day become a head basketball coach. I traded salary for the more valuable lifetime experience. The bottom line for me was simple—I valued my passion and dream for a basketball career over making more money. It was more important for me to try to achieve my long-term goals rather than focusing on financial gain. More money would have given material things to the person I already was, not the person I truly wanted to be.

Brainstorming My Values: Seven Questions

Not all decisions, however, come down to money and passion. You will have to dig deep and brainstorm to help find *your* personal core values. Answer the questions below to help discover your guiding principles. *I've shared my answers to give you examples.*

1. When are you the most inspired?
   - *I'm most inspired when I'm around positive, fun, loyal, curious, honest, dependable, team-oriented, and energized people.*

2. What gives you purpose?
   - *Helping other people commit to personal growth gives me purpose.*

3. How do you spend your free time?
   - *I spend my free time enjoying my family members as well as reading and writing about personal growth.*

4. What do you do with your discretionary money?
   - *I spend my discretionary money on self-help books and seminars.*

5. Who do you look up to?
   - *I look up to speakers and authors.*

6. What do you think about when you're by yourself?
   - *I think about investing time and pouring personal growth and development into other people.*

7. What would you die for?
   - *I would die for my faith and family.*

STOP Brainstorming Your Values: Seven Questions

Answer the questions below to help discover your core values. Be honest with yourself, because this is a significant step for growth.

1. When are you the most inspired?

2. What gives you purpose?

3. How do you spend your free time?

4. What do you do with your discretionary money?

5. Who do you look up to?

6. What do you think about when you're by yourself?

7. What would you die for?

My Values Brain Dump

Now that you've brainstormed your values, it's time to make sure that you have all possible values on the table before you start the selection process. When I did this exercise, I listed the following twenty-one values:

1. Faith	8. Loyalty	15. Curiosity
2. Family	9. Dependability	16. Time
3. Friends	10. Execution	17. Passions
4. Fun	11. Wellness	18. Giving
5. Education	12. Honesty	19. Love
6. Writing	13. Energy	20. Teamwork
7. Thinking	14. Inspiration	21. Attitude

STOP Your Values Brain-Dump

In no particular order, start listing your possible values. Don't over think this. To make your list, brain dump your answers from the previous seven questions. If you're struggling to find your values, just write down what's important to you in your life.

1.	8.	15.
2.	9.	16.
3.	10.	17.
4.	11.	18.
5.	12.	19.
6.	13.	20.
7.	14.	21.

Rating My Top Values

Next, it's important to rate each of the possible values that you brain dumped. Through this process, I realized that three of my values really stood out, with many of the other considerations seeming to fall underneath them. Below are my top three values of equal importance.

1. Attitude
2. Passions

    a. Relationships – Faith, Family, Friends, Colleagues
    b. Wellness – Food, Exercise, Water, Sleep
    c. Personal Growth – Reading, Writing, Thinking, Sharing, Applying

3. Execution

🛑 Rating Your Top Values

As you've seen, there are countless types of values. Now it's your turn to choose the ones that are right for you. Rate each of the possible values that you brain dumped on a scale of 1-10, with 1 being not important to you and 10 being very important to you. Then, rank and select your top three to six values.

1.
2.
3.
4.
5.
6.

My Values Definitions

Once you have identified your most important values, it's imperative to define each one in your own words because they just might be with you forever. Here are my examples.

1. Attitude –My way of thinking that makes or breaks me.
2. Passions – My desires that point me in the right direction toward fulfilling my ideal life.
3. Execution – My time spent on activities that allow me to achieve my values, passions, and vision.

STOP Your Values Definitions

Write your own definition of each of your top three to six values, focusing on what each value means to you.

1.
2.
3.
4.
5.
6.

Your Stated Values: Pause, Review, and Reflect

- What did you learn while prioritizing your values?
- Do your values match with the ones suggested by the organizations at which you work, belong, or volunteer?
- Are your values similar to those of your family, friends, or coworkers?
- Where do your values come from?
- How much time have you spent on your values in the last week?

🛑 Blending Your Values with Your Ideal Day

Now that you've identified your core values, rewrite your ideal day in light of them. Compare and contrast your values to the ideal day that you wrote about in the introduction. What do you have to start and/or stop doing to be more mindful of your values, or to make them more present? What *SHIFTS* do you have to make to your day so you can start on your path to living your ideal life?

_____

_____

_____

_____

_____

Concentrate on living your values day by day. **Incorporating your values into your day will gradually increase the amount of time you'll spend living your ideal day.** Keep your values visible so you can intentionally evaluate each day with respect to those values.

How Will You Feel at Age Seventy-Five?

Remembering that day in 2003, I'm so glad that my parents asked me, "Money aside, which option would give you the most experience in the area that you ultimately want to work in for the long run?" Sacrificing short-term compensation pointed me in the right direction to focus on my long-term passion.

How will you feel at age seventy-five when you're looking back and reminiscing on life? Will you look back with regret or with pride? Don't let an opportunity pass you by, as it may only come once in a lifetime. It was the author and a pioneer of the self-help movement, James Allen, who once said, **"He who would accomplish little must sacrifice little; he who would achieve much must sacrifice much."**

The Heart of Everything

If you're still feeling stressed and burned out, that's ok. It's going to take some hard work to go on this journey. Clarifying what's most important to you is just the start to redirecting your life. In your head, picture a ladder. The ground represents your personal core values or foundation. The top rung represents your fulfilled life. The middle rungs represent everything that you'll do to climb toward creating a smoother journey to living your ideal life right now...if you keep your personal values at the heart of everything you do.

Now that you've shifted into Gear One, it's time to build on your foundational core values. In Gear Two, you'll learn that growth is vital for everyone. If we're not growing, we're decaying. In the next chapter, I'll reveal my *Move to Grow* principle that will lead you to your cues and transform your life. Once personal growth becomes a daily ritual, you'll be on the fast track, and nothing will stop you.

"Foundation" Key Moves

- Brain dump your possible values.
- Rate and form your top values.
- Define each of your values.
- Keep your values visible.
- Blend your values with your ideal day.

STOP **Write down the *first thing* from this chapter's content that you will move to act on.**

_____

_____

_____

_____

_____

SHIFT Roadmap: From Foundation to Principle

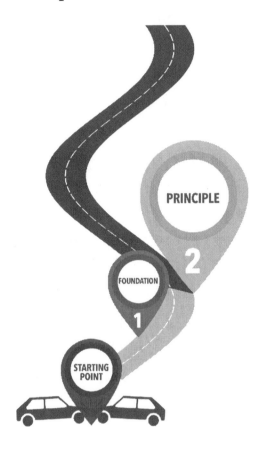

CHAPTER TWO

PRINCIPLE:
PURSUE PERSONAL GROWTH

"Don't wish it was easier, wish you were better.
Don't wish for less problems, wish for more skills.
Don't wish for less challenge, wish for more wisdom."

– Jim Rohn

It was the Fourth of July in 1996 on the lakefront of Manitowoc, Wisconsin. I had just turned sixteen and couldn't wait to get behind the wheel of my first vehicle, a 1988 5-speed Nissan Sentra. I was driving with a few of my closest friends and family members when I came to a stop light. As soon as the light turned green, I casually released the clutch—but I released it too fast. The engine stalled, and we all felt a bit of whiplash. Trying to regain my confidence in front of everyone, I turned the ignition on and tried again. Nothing changed, and I was still stuck in the same predicament. The fireworks had just ended, so we were sitting in bumper-to-bumper traffic. This wasn't the best time for my engine to stall at least forty times.

To this day, I can recall the distinct sound of what seemed like hundreds of honking car horns. When I finally cleared the intersection, I decided to take the scenic route home and get as far away as I could from that mess. Prior to my Nissan, I had only driven automatic transmission cars with my parents while learning to drive. So no big surprise, driving with three pedals and a shifter was a bit of a challenge for me in the beginning. Rather than giving up out of frustration, I finally realized that I needed to carefully engage the clutch to move forward.

When I Started Moving, I Started Growing

When I finally arrived home later that evening, I was thinking about how I ever got into that mess, and the answer was simple. I needed to *Move to Grow*. In that situation, I had to properly engage the clutch and *SHIFT* gears to move forward in my manual transmission car—and the very same concept applies if you want to move forward in life. Unfortunately, most of us live our lives with our RPMs revved up to the max while we're still stuck in a low gear. Our pure lack of understanding of how to *SHIFT* our engines into a different gear leaves our engines screaming and our gears maxed out without productive movement forward. We don't always realize that we need to *SHIFT*, so we are living but not really going anywhere. We are standing still, remaining stagnant, and not living up to our fullest potential. Do you ever feel like you're so busy going a million MPH, but not heading anywhere?

A couple of weeks after the incident, I learned to *SHIFT* correctly by easing down the clutch and shifting into the next gear. Literally, shifting gears made me feel that I was doing far more than just driving: I was moving toward something that I *wanted* to do. When I was sixteen, I *wanted* to play basketball at the gym to get better and I *wanted* to go to the sporting card shop to learn how to buy and sell cards. I was moving and growing.

Within our everyday lives, the very same concept applies. Every one of us must *SHIFT* through speeds—both in work and life—to move toward our future success and happiness; otherwise, we don't go anywhere and we're stuck sitting in our cars in the driveway.

Move to Grow Principle Revealed

Plain and simple—if you don't commit to personal growth, you won't move and grow. You'll remain stuck in a rut, instead of living to your potential. Thirteen years after that embarrassing Independence Day in 1996, I put my gear into neutral and thought to myself, "If I had to choose a couple of things that would render the highest results for me, they'd be moving and growing because you have to do both to accomplish just about anything." Thus, I developed the *Move to Grow* principle, which asserts that "all growth starts with personal growth." Personal growth is the mindful pursuit of self-improvement by expanding knowledge and improving skills.

> All growth starts with personal growth.

Knowing this helped me bridge the gap from where I was to where I wanted to be. The *Move to Grow* principle will do the same for you, as long as you make time for this life-changing priority. Personal growth is the fundamental habit to find and live a fulfilled life...if you put the principle into practice. Pursue personal growth now, and you'll be one step closer to achieving what you desire.

Why Did I Wait 13 Years to *Move to Grow?*

Unfortunately, I didn't know how to grow. Yes, you read that correctly. I had no clue that personal growth existed. It was a process that took me time to learn.

In 2007 and 2008, I was living in Utah and working as the director of player development for the University of Utah men's basketball team. When Rachel and I arrived in 2007, it was a new beginning and we were excited. I had moved Rachel across the country for my dream. The head coach and his wife were friends of ours. Basketball was everything to me professionally.

Fast forward six months...I was no longer excited about or focused on winning. Instead, my focus and desire was about moving on. The defining moment for me happened on January 22, 2008, when our team was playing against New Mexico at The Pit arena. It was a great game in an iconic arena, but we ended up losing by a mere ten points. Immediately after the game, I recall feeling a pit (no pun intended) growing in my stomach. The players and coaches were devastated. I was truly miserable. Something inside me was screaming out that it just wasn't right. I finally realized that this wasn't my dream anymore. It was my second crash. My temporary solution of moving from one team to another was no longer *the* solution. If I truly wanted to be happy in my life, I needed to make a move. I just knew I had to initiate a change.

The Best Interview Question of All Time

After searching for various positions in the greater Milwaukee area in the spring of 2008, I quickly landed an interview at the Wisconsin Athletic Club (WAC) for a general manager position. During the job interview, one of the owners of the WAC, Chez Misko, asked me, "Derek, what is your plan for personal development?" Being slightly caught off guard by the question, I decided to wing it, thinking I could figure it out as I went along. I remember how I rambled on and on for a good three to four minutes, talking in circles about how hard I worked. It was like I was running on a treadmill—not going anywhere, though the speed and intensity were increasing with each passing minute and I was quickly running out of energy.

I mentioned how passionate I was about the job, and that I'd be a great employee if they would take a chance on me. I even said that my dream was *always* to be the manager of a gym…which was never the case. At no point in my rambling, incoherent speech was there anything relevant that had anything to do with personal development at all. Ever since that brief moment in time, the idea of implementing a plan for personal growth and development has been foremost in my mind.

Hooked from a Book

Even though I believe I botched that interview question, I ended up receiving an offer from the WAC. Soon after, I accepted the position, and we moved back to our home state of Wisconsin. Within my first year, my former colleague and dear mentor, Deb Orr, recommended the previously mentioned book by international leadership guru, John C. Maxwell. The book was titled *The 21 Irrefutable Laws of Leadership*. From that day forward, I was officially hooked on the journey to personal development.

To my surprise, I learned that initially, Maxwell had also struggled to grow. He also had a mentor who introduced him to leadership, just like I had. Although I didn't realize it at the time, Deb was acting as a mentor and facilitating my growth by sharing this excellent resource book. In retrospect, my decision to join the WAC was the best career decision that I've ever made because of the ongoing commitment to learning and development emphasized at the executive level of the organization. Today, my drive for personal growth is a part of my daily routine. It's my hope that *SHIFT* will hook you on this incredible journey.

A Look Under the Hood by Deb Orr, Derek's Mentor

Lucky for me, I was on the other side of that table in the job interview where Derek pounded his fist and said, "I care." That fist pound proved to be prophetic. He's the real deal. And I feel pretty good about helping to spot it. Most people are taken in by his looks and obvious skills and talents. Very few, I suspect, know what's under that impressive-looking hood. Wise beyond his years, he possesses a quiet determination and relentless drive to improve coupled with the discipline of an elite athlete. His research and preparation are legendary (often to the dismay of less prepared colleagues). But what I'm particularly amazed about after reading this book is his willingness to be vulnerable and let *everyone* see under the hood. Who knew? And here's the thing; we all have stuff. We all crash. In the words of another of my favorite authors, Brene Brown, "If you are brave enough, often enough, you *will* fail." The question becomes, what do you do? It's always easier to do nothing, but don't kid yourself, that is a decision, too. Would you rather crash and burn or crash and *SHIFT*? Caution: there is work involved. But you have a "fellow traveler" in Derek. You won't be disappointed. It took me three days to write one paragraph...do the math. Lucky for you, he persevered to the finish line of his book.

 ## Your Growth Guide

Identify someone who has contributed to your personal growth. Write down his or her name and the type of help you received. Finally, send that person a thank you message via text, email, or (ideally) handwritten note.

_____

_____

_____

_____

_____

I Wasn't the Only One Who Was Clueless

A couple of years after I started committing to personal growth, I walked into a huge bookstore and asked one of the employees where the personal growth section was located. He gave me a blank stare. He didn't know where the section was and he worked there! Oddly enough, the personal growth section was within fifty feet of him. This was a defining moment for me. I came to the harsh realization that *many* people don't know what personal growth is, or what personal growth means. Clearly, those who don't know what it is or what it means also don't take the necessary steps each day to integrate personal growth into their lives. It's vital for them to be exposed to personal development in order to be intentional in pursuing it. Congratulations…with *SHIFT*, you've already taken the first step.

What Does It Really Mean to Grow?

It was eleven-time NBA Champion, Bill Russell, of the Boston Celtics who once said, **"Work to become, not to acquire."** True to his word, Russell became more and grew as a basketball player before, during, and after the championships. He never stopped his steady progress, and he never had a finish line. Personal growth implies that you want to get better at something. If you continually pursue personal growth, you'll always be moving and improving.

Ask yourself this: are you getting better every day, especially in the areas that you love? I call this the One Percent Rule, which drives you to become one percent better every single day. For me, I've learned to rise early in the morning to find time to work on my personal development. Without this early morning routine, I wouldn't be growing. Just as Bill Russell never stopped growing, we should all strive to improve ourselves. There is more to every stage in life than getting older. Moving to grow and getting better at anything is a never-ending journey. Even in the tech-savvy world that surrounds each of us today, personal growth is a timeless trend.

> There is more to every stage in life than getting older.

Why Should You Grow?

A lot of people will tell you that it's important to grow, but why is it important? There really is no right or easy answer. Just like there isn't one definition of success, we all have our own personal benefits and reasons to grow. You will want to grow for *your own* reasons that matter to you alone. Your personal reasons for growth might be entirely different than mine. There is no standard formula for everyone.

How Has Personal Growth Helped Me?

Here are the top fifteen benefits from ongoing personal growth that have helped me and continue to help me since I became hooked. Personal growth helps me...

1. Be a better dad and husband
2. Understand myself better
3. Increase my confidence
4. Find my passions
5. Create my ideal life right now
6. Write and speak
7. Fight through tough times
8. Be healthier
9. Move from being a boss to being a leader
10. Earn promotions at work
11. Make more money
12. Find more growth-minded friends
13. Strengthen my faith
14. Reach my potential
15. Help others grow and develop

Focusing on personal growth has worked wonders in my life. Looking back, I don't know how I survived before my self-discipline.

What Will Motivate You to Grow?

Take a moment and write down some ways that you expect personal growth to help you now and into the future. *Feel free to include any ways that personal growth has already helped you in the past.* Don't worry. Your list is not set in stone. It'll *SHIFT* as you grow.

- •
- •
- •
- •
- •
- •

·   ·   ·
·   ·   ·
·   ·   ·

How do you feel after writing down your benefits and reasons to grow? Are you inspired to commit to personal growth? Even though our lists may look completely different, here is what I know will be the same: we both want to create positive change in our lives. I've invested time to write this book. You've invested time to read this book. **The best way to change is to grow...and this is just the beginning.** Writing these down will help to motivate you.

Why *Shouldn't* You Grow?

There are many factors to think about and consider while you pursue personal growth. There is, however, one thing that should *not* be part of your motivation. Don't even bother to push yourself to grow and achieve if your actual goal is only to be better than everyone else. If you try to be better than everyone else, you'll create competitions that you'll never win. Somebody will always be better than you at something. Somebody will always have more than you do. Grow to be the best that *you* can be, so you can help others be the best that *they* can be.

> Grow to be the best that *you* can be, so you can help others be the best that *they* can be.

My Trail of Cues

Looking back to the day I committed to personal growth, I had inspiring cues *before* that moment, which pointed me in the direction of personal growth. Failing as a speaker, feeling frustrated as a basketball coach, receiving an interview at the WAC, and being asked about my plan for personal development all contributed to this moment.

Additionally, I had a trail of cues *during* my initial commitment to personal growth. I was given the gift of the self-help book from a mentor, I received personal development articles in my inbox, and I attended workshops at athletic club industry conventions.

The signs continued. I had more affirming moments *after* committing to personal growth. I volunteered to lead the new-hire orientation at the WAC, I was asked to teach leadership classes at Wisconsin Lutheran College, and I was promoted to lead the training and development department at the WAC.

Today, I continue to have more cues and positive confirmation that personal growth is right for me…such as being asked to coach others, obtaining positive feedback on my **DerekDeprey.com/DerekBlog** articles, and continually expanding my speaking and coaching business.

So you see? I had hints all along. I just wasn't aware of them until well after they began. I had a mix of exuberant, unpleasant, and thought-provoking experiences. Some of my cues were quick moments of taking the initiative to get uncomfortable and make things happen.

I focused on all the cues before, during, and after beginning my journey of personal growth and have come to the realization that I had to step out of my comfort zone to confront my big fears. You can do the same, and I will go along with you.

🛑 Your Trail of Cues

It's time to slow down now, with the goal of ultimately speeding up. Take a moment and reflect so that you can become more aware of the cues that signal you to be more intentional about personal growth. Write down some of the past and current signs that pointed and point you in the direction to *Move to Grow*.

Past Cues

-
-
-
-
-

Current Cues

-
-
-
-
-

Now that you can physically see your cues, are you feeling less stuck and more energized?

Follow the Cues that Get You Excited

When you were reflecting about your cues, did you have moments of excitement? Moments of disappointment? Did you have a mix of both? As you've seen, my path to personal growth had and continues to have a mix of both excitement and disappointment. Every experience, good or bad, led me to where I am today. Follow your cues that get you excited about personal growth. If you do, you'll be on fire with energy and enthusiasm.

You Didn't Suddenly Wake Up with Passion

Don't be frustrated if you don't yet know what you're passionate about. Looking back, I didn't suddenly find passion. I committed to the path of consistent personal growth. I realized what excited me the most, which was speaking, teaching, writing, and reading. Today, I try to spend as much time as I can enjoying those things. **How can you turn personal growth into fun?**

Your Fear Will Diminish

I'll never forget the time when a colleague walked into my office and said, "Derek, some employees think that you're wasting our time with all of this personal development stuff that you do." After hearing this comment, I took a deep breath. Thankfully, I didn't get defensive because I learned from a few mentors that not everyone wants to learn and grow. Unfortunately, most people don't grow for one simple reason: fear. If this is you, your fear will diminish over time as you move through this book. When finished, you'll have the tools to step out of your comfort zone. Nothing worth having comes easy.

I'm Your Fellow Traveler...Let's Drive Together

Now that I've been on the personal growth journey for quite some time, I'm asked daily, "Derek, will you have coffee or lunch with me and teach me how to grow?" Since I'm unable to meet with everyone who expresses interest, I wrote this book to impact their growth and development.

If you've made it this far, congratulations on your burning desire to *Move to Grow*. You're special. If you're still a little bit afraid, don't worry. I'm on the fulfillment journey with you as your fellow traveler.

Are You Going or Growing through Life?

I can hear some of you saying right now, "But Derek, I'm too busy to grow." People never cease to complain about their busy schedules. Don't grow after you have kids. Don't grow after you quit your job. Don't grow after you have more money. Don't grow after you read this book. The word "after" is a self-defeating word. Take action now! **Don't go through life. Grow through it!**

Personal Growth Starts with You

Be intentional. Simply make a conscious decision to *Move to Grow*. Personal growth doesn't start with an item; it starts with you. **You are the CEO of your life.** Move out of your own way. Block off some time to develop yourself and to work strategically on developing the rest of your life. Making this a part of your day, just like anything else, will make life better. Growth is lifelong. Growth is fulfilling.

You're Growing, but Where Are You Going?

Now that you've shifted into Gear Two and made a mental decision to grow, it's time to *SHIFT* into Gear Three and get a specific idea of where you're headed. In the next chapter, you'll visualize your preferred future and think about how you want the world to be different. You'll create a vision that will give you the motivation for the choices you'll make on your journey of moving from frustrated to fulfilled.

"Principle" Key Moves

- Thank a person who has contributed to your personal growth.
- Think about your reasons and motivations to grow.
- Follow the cues that get you excited.
- Commit to the *Move to Grow* principle.

STOP **Write down the *first thing* from this chapter's content that you will move to act on.**

_____

_____

_____

_____

_____

SHIFT Roadmap: From Principle to Vision

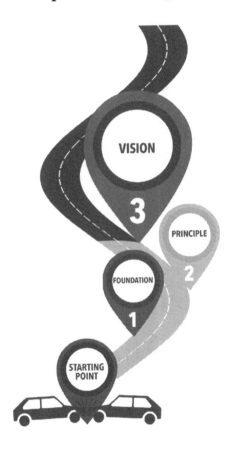

CHAPTER THREE

VISION:
VISUALIZE YOUR PREFERRED FUTURE

"The only thing worse than being
blind is having sight but no vision."
– Helen Keller

Whenever I think of vision, I think about my family's Disney World vacation, and being at Cinderella's Castle. When I visited once, I saw that inside the castle's archway are a number of large mosaic murals that tell the story of Cinderella. As I gazed at the creation, I remembered overhearing a cast member telling another guest that the artwork was made with about 300,000 tiny pixels of glass in over 500 different colors.

From Frustration Pixels to Fulfillment Pixels

This got me thinking about the cast members who shaped the masterpiece. I'm sure that they started their undertaking feeling totally overwhelmed with so many random pieces! With time and determination, they visualized their desired image, and ultimately found joy and fulfillment with the end result.

Do you feel overwhelmed or frustrated by the thought of all your pixels or to-dos? Do you even know where to start, or is your vision hard to see?

From 1984–1986, I wanted to be a popstar like Michael Jackson. From 1987–1989, I wanted to play in the NFL. From 1990–1993, I wanted to own a sports card shop. From 1994–1995, I wanted to be a star high school athlete like my sister, Shann Stephani. From 1996–1998, I wanted to play on the historic MECCA floor for the state high school basketball tournament. From 1999–2000, I wanted to play Division I basketball. From 2001–2007, I wanted to be a Division I head basketball coach. From 2008–2014, I wanted to be a CEO. In 2015, I wanted to start and own a speaking business to move others to grow.

Some of you might be wondering why my visions or dreams changed so often. They changed because I changed. Thankfully, my values and cues led me, and continue to lead me, in the right direction. Growth and development helps us all to understand ourselves better. It will stretch your dreams, and hopefully move you toward your vision. When you know your desired vision, your pixels or to-dos will be less frustrating and more fulfilling.

What Is Vision?

Knowing your core values and committing to the *Move to Grow* principle will only take you so far. Vision refers to your preferred future or lifetime goals. It's like seeing the light at the end of the tunnel. Before you go from where you are to where you want to be, it's important to have a simple picture or, at the very least, a general idea of where you are going in your life. Think "what," not "how."

Here are some real-life vision examples:

- My CPR teacher who sees more saved lives making a difference in the world.
- My carpenter dad who sees many happy families enjoying their homes.
- My barista who sees miles of people connecting with each other in the community.

Why Is Vision Important?

Having vision leads to fulfillment. Vision has the ability to outlive you. Knowing your vision is important for three major reasons.

1. **Vision gives you purpose beyond yourself**...it touches the hearts of other people.
2. **Vision can turn a "have to" into a "want to"**...it serves as motivation for the choices that you'll eventually make during your *SHIFT*.
3. **Vision gives you direction**...if you want to get things done, know where you want to go with your life.

Only with vision are you able to look out the windshield and work toward creating a plan around achieving it. You must dream it to live it.

Where Am I Now?

Before I share my vision, it's important that I think about my current location with respect to that vision. In other words, where am I now? Right now, I'm saying yes to too many things outside my personal vision, passions, and priorities. (See "From Frustrated" circle in the *Move to Grow* in Action diagram.)

What Is My Vision?

Because I know my current location, I can now consider my vision. To help me decide my vision, I asked myself, "With respect to my core values, how do I want the world to be different?" My vision: I will help to move one million people from frustrated to fulfilled through books, keynotes, workshops, and coaching. (See "To Fulfilled" circle in the *Move to Grow* in Action diagram.)

Move to Grow in Action by Derek

FROM FRUSTRATED:
I'm saying yes to too many things outside my personal vision, passions, and priorities

TO FULFILLED:
I will help to move one million people from frustrated to fulfilled through books, keynotes, workshops, and coaching

STOP Where Are *You* Now?

With respect to your desired vision, where are you now? What is your current location? Reflect and write. This activity could take you five minutes or five days. For example, your current location might be that many of the colleagues you lead are burning out because they spend too much time on projects that expose their weaknesses. When you're ready, write your name in the blank line above your *Move to Grow* diagram. Then, transfer your "Where are you now" statement into your "From Frustrated" circle below.

_____

_____

_____

_____

_____

STOP What Is *Your* Vision?

Where do you want to be? What's your vision or preferred future? With no distractions, reflect and write. For example, your vision might be to create and lead a dream team where everyone is playing to their strengths. When you're ready, transfer your vision into the "To Fulfilled" circle below.

_____

_____

_____

_____

_____

If you run out of space, keep in mind that Abraham Lincoln wrote the Gettysburg Address, one of the best-known speeches in American history, in 272 words.

Move to Grow in Action by _____

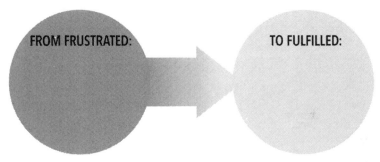

🛑 How Do You Want the World to Be Different?

Was that tough? It was for me. Just because vision is supposed to be a clear picture, it does not mean that nailing it down on paper is easy. If you're struggling to write down your vision, really stop and reflect this time. What if the biggest gift we can give the world is to be our best selves? How then would the world be different? Look back to your values and cues from earlier. Does your vision align?

> What if the biggest gift we can give the world is to be our best selves?

Are you being led in a specific direction? If you were gone today, what's the one thing that you wish you would have fixed?

If you're still unsure that what you wrote down is really your vision, don't worry. I didn't decide my vision on day one, either. This chapter is intentionally short because you'll find clarity and have the ability to tweak your vision as you *SHIFT* through the gears. Just get started and be honest with yourself. Be willing to see yourself as fulfilled.

It's Time to Go APE

Now that you've confronted your deepest frustrations, formed your core values, made the decision to pursue personal growth, and visualized your preferred future, it's time to actually grow. Gear Four outlines the formula, **APE: A**ttitude + **P**assions + **E**xecution = Growth. APE represents the vehicle between you and your vision. Each part of the formula will have its own respective chapter. In the next chapter, you'll get an overview. APE is all about having the right attitude while finding your passions and priorities as well as taking the necessary actions to move your life forward! Once this formula is implemented into your everyday life, you'll be well on your way to reaching your true potential.

Where are you heading?

"Vision" Key Moves

- Recognize that vision gives you direction.
- Become aware of your current location.
- Determine your vision.

To find your current location or where you are now, take the complimentary *SHIFT*ability Assessment. To get started, please visit **DerekDeprey.com/ShiftBookResources**

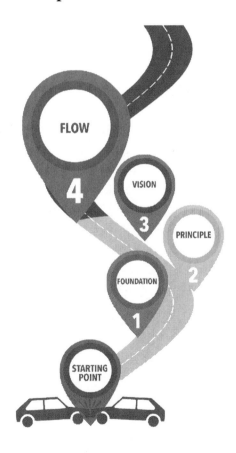 **Write down the *first thing* from this chapter's content that you will move to act on.**

_____

_____

_____

_____

_____

SHIFT Roadmap: From Vision to Flow

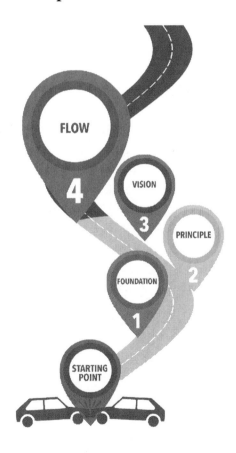

CHAPTER FOUR

FLOW:
FOLLOW THE APE FORMULA

"Be clear about your goal,
but be flexible about the process of achieving it."
– Brian Tracy

H ave you ever been part of an organization-wide technology software upgrade? If you have, you know how stressful things can be. In the early fall of 2014, the Wisconsin Athletic Club decided it was time to upgrade. We were going from the heavy, bogged-down, paper-based system of the 1980s to the light, efficient, paperless world of the 2010s.

By late fall of the same year, implementation time was growing closer. Our CEO, Ray O'Connor, scheduled a meeting with me to discuss the upcoming change. During our conversation, he asked me two questions that I'll never forget. First, he asked, "Derek, would you be willing to help lead the flow of this transformation with a talented team?" Even though I was still unclear as to what I would specifically be doing, I quickly said "Yes." Second, Ray asked, "Do you realize that this is going to be a messier project than you're used to, but it'll be good for you?"

After pausing, glancing at my notes, and then quickly pondering what in the world I just got myself into, I asked a clarifying question: "What do you mean by flow and transformation?" He responded, "Let me back up. In corporate America, many people use the words process and change. There seems to be a bit of a negative reaction to both words. When I felt that reaction, I substituted the word flow for process, and the word transformation for change. To me, these look and feel more positive. What are your thoughts?"

[*Before I share my thoughts to Ray's response, it's important that I provide a little bit of background information about myself. In 2008, about a month after I started my new career, I was asked to take a self-assessment about communication styles. The four communication styles were Action, Process, People, and Idea. The result of my assessment was "Process," which meant I was mostly into strategies, organization, and facts... I was inflexible.*]

Initially, I said to myself, "I hate messes and don't want to take on this nine-month project." How did I respond to Ray? "I'm in!" It was time to get uncomfortable to help push myself and transform our organization.

My *New* Communication Style: Self-Assessment Results

Because most people assumed I was mostly process oriented, I decided to retake the self-assessment before the project started. What was the result? I was "People" dominant. Eight years after the first self-assessment, I had made a 180 degree *SHIFT* from strategies, organization, and facts to communication, relationships, and teamwork. Was the transformation of the project perfect? No, far from it. We did, however, successfully complete the implementation. I'm forever thankful that I grew my abilities in communication, relationships, and teamwork before the project, because I couldn't have led the flow without doing so.

Flow and Process

You might be thinking, "How did you grow?" Before I reveal the formula, let's dig a little deeper and explore the words flow and process. Flow is the action of moving along steadily and continuously. Flow represents a river that effortlessly adjusts to rock and other obstacles that might be in the way. This doesn't mean we simply go with the flow; instead, it means there isn't only one path. Process is a series of actions or steps taken to achieve a particular end. In other words, there's only one way.

Overall, I like processes. From my experience, just about anything successful comes from a good process. In fact, it takes a process for us to move, breathe, and think. I could go on and on.

Looking back, however, Ray's use of the word flow vs. process was brilliant. Why? Because there are too many bad processes that are forced, and too few good processes that actually flow.

Bad processes are complicated and rigid. They burn people out with numerous approval steps from the top down. Can you relate? Good processes, on the other hand, are simple and flexible. They help people be more efficient and effective. Put rather simply, good processes flow. What are some of your good processes?

Follow the APE Formula:
Attitude + Passions + Execution = Growth

Let's rewind to chapter one for a moment. We spent some time brainstorming personal values. Remember, all my research from other experts in the self-help field led me to discover one major aha—the formulas for success narrowed down to just a few very simple concepts that are identical to my personal core values of Attitude, Passions, and Execution. A few years after that discovery, I went to work and developed my own formula for growth, which is APE: Attitude + Passions + Execution = Growth. APE results in growth.

> APE: Attitude + Passions + Execution = Growth.

The Vehicle to Your Vision

The formula of Attitude, Passions, and Execution is a simple, yet powerful tool for growth if it's used correctly. By correctly, I mean having the right attitude, finding your passions, and executing the necessary actions to move forward in life. If you can successfully use APE, there is no doubt that you'll be driving in the right vehicle toward your desired vision.

Once this formula is implemented into your daily life, I can assure you that you will notice big changes. Positive attitudes and thoughts will produce positive results in your life. You'll find yourself much happier throughout the day as you exercise positive thinking. You'll find yourself being much more efficient with your time when you learn to successfully prioritize what is important in your life... your passions. And finally, the greatest gap in the world is the gap between *knowing* and *doing*. It's simply not enough to know your passions and maintain a positive attitude. You must also execute.

But does the formula follow a specific order?

The Three-Legged Stool

Do you know why farmers use a three-legged stool to milk? It is because the stool can be used on any surface and will be sturdy. Visualize a three-legged stool with each of the legs named Attitude, Passions, and Execution. The three-legged APE stool can be used in any situation, with any person, to provide a solid base and achieve results.

When assembling a three-legged stool, the legs can be assembled in any order. Attitude, Passions, and Execution do *not* have to work in a linear motion. As you've seen from my examples, I often flip-flopped Passions and Execution to make Attitude + Execution + Passions = Growth. In other words, I "Executed" my way into discovering my cues and finding my "Passions." You must adapt APE to your unique situation.

When removing any leg of a three-legged stool, the stool will fall. You need all three to function.

Unity

Attitude, Passions, and Execution have equal importance. You need all three to grow and reach your vision or potential. The diagram below best illustrates the unity between Attitude, Passions, and Execution

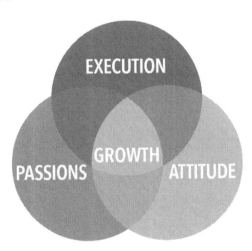

Actually Change Your Behavior

I'm often asked, "Derek, how do you actually change behavior?" If this is you, think back to your vision statement. Ask yourself,

"Will I *enjoy* the day-to-day activities necessary to achieve my vision?" In other words, "Would I be fulfilled performing those day-to-day activities for the rest of my life?" If so, you are on the path to achieving your preferred future, and APE will help get you there more quickly. If not, APE will help you find a better way to change direction.

Whenever my daughters go to their grandparents' house, they like to ride the horses, Thunder and Lightning. Naturally, they want to hop on and start riding right away. We did quickly learn, however, that it doesn't work that way. Before riding, horses should be groomed, tied safely for saddling, lunged, and mounted. The point is, if your vision is to be a horseback rider, then you must enjoy the entire journey, including the prep work, because you're literally not going anywhere for a while. **The goal is not just to enjoy the preferred future, but also to take pleasure in APE each and every day.**

Think Marathon, Not Sprint

I'd be lying if I said that APE is easy, because it's not. If you have a profound desire to be of use, to learn and to grow right up until the day you die, you'll find APE an invigorating challenge that will keep you on your toes for many years to come. Like running a marathon, the flow of APE will vary from person to person as it relates to goals, times, energy levels, or training routines.

One element won't vary, regardless of what your vision might be.

If your vision is to be fit, then you must have the long-term discipline to eat better and exercise. If your vision is to have an amazing garden, then you must have the long-term discipline to pull weeds and water flowers. If your vision is to make more money, then you must have the long-term discipline to grow and develop.

Do you see a pattern? Long-term discipline. You have a choice: the dedication of discipline to achieve your vision or the pain of regret when you lose it.

Do You Want to BE Successful or STAY Successful?

You see, there are a lot of books written about how to be successful. Unfortunately, there are not a lot of books written about how to stay successful. Think to yourself: do you want to "be" successful or "stay" successful? If you want to *be* successful, feel the pain of regret and only do APE for a day. If you want to *stay* successful, choose the dedication of discipline and practice APE forever.

> If you want to *be* successful, feel the pain of regret and only do APE for a day. If you want to *stay* successful, choose the dedication of discipline and practice APE forever.

Bit by Bit, a Bit Will Become Big

APE is a long-term solution that will become easier over time and will deliver long-lasting results. The results from this process will be similar to the results from becoming healthier. Most likely, you won't see success in days or weeks. You will, however, see progress in months…and breakthroughs in years.

For example, let's take the flow of this book. (By the way, if you want a messy project with no exact flow in your life, write a book.) I woke up every day at 5:00 a.m. and worked on it for two hours, including weekends, for two straight years. After the first few days, I didn't think I'd ever finish. But after the first few months, I knew it had become a reality. During the journey of writing this book, I kept thinking to myself, "Bit by bit, a bit will become big."

I know 100 percent that APE works because I've been applying it to my life since 2008. When I first started, everything changed—I mean everything! I'm rarely grumpy, behind, exhausted, stressed, impatient, irritable, or unfocused. I've seen it work miracles, not just in my life, but in the lives of others. But it's not enough to tell you…I'm going to show you.

APE's Archrival and Nemesis...You?

It may surprise you to hear me say this, but it's important to mention that APE doesn't work for everyone. Why not? Because attitude, passions, and execution are controlled 100 percent by you, and you may decide to go in a different direction.

1. *You* can choose to have or to keep your bad attitude toward personal growth.
2. *You* can choose to ignore your passions.
3. *You* can choose to execute things that drain you rather than things that put you on the path to fulfillment.

If you want to grow, try to minimize or avoid these enemies at all costs.

The Best Is Yet to Come

There are three things that you have the power to control: Attitude, Passions, and Execution. Now that you've been given a rudimentary explanation of APE, it's time to breakdown each concept. We'll stay in Gear Four for the next three chapters to ensure that you don't get stuck on the shoulder of the road. In the next chapter, you'll learn how to adopt a positive mindset. No matter what your personal definition of success is, you must have the right attitude to achieve it. Attitude is your engine for growth. Stop your downward spiral once and for all. Today is the day that you will choose to have a positive and impassioned attitude. Opening yourself up to this change in attitude will help facilitate your desire to change your behavior.

Continue flowing. The best is yet to come.

"Flow" Key Moves

- Understand that APE results in growth.
- Adapt the APE formula to meet your wants and needs.
- Appreciate the messy journey toward fulfillment.
- Choose long-term discipline.
- Be somewhat patient.

Remember...you get what you put in. If you want to truly move from frustrated to fulfilled, then you must finish the book. If you get stuck, I'm here to help. Join my Shifting Gears Team private experience, and I'll coach you through the journey. For more information, please visit **DerekDeprey.com/ShiftingGearsTeam**

STOP **Write down the *first thing* from this chapter's content that you will move to act on.**

_____

_____

_____

_____

_____

SHIFT Roadmap: From Flow to Attitude

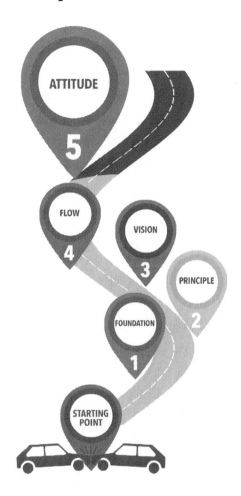

CHAPTER FIVE

ATTITUDE:
ADOPT A POSITIVE MINDSET

*"The greatest discovery of any generation is that a
human being can alter his life by altering his attitude."*

– William James

Have you ever taken a college readiness assessment exam?
In 1997, when I was a junior in high school, I took the
American College Test (ACT). I don't actually remember
physically taking the test. I do remember, however, receiving my
composite score of 19 out of 36 in the mail. I was embarrassed,
plain and simple. In fact, until now, no one outside of my parents,
high school guidance counselor, and my friend who had asked,
"Are you sure you want to put that story in your book?" knew my
score. This is the first time that I've talked about it.

When I arrived at school the next day, everyone was talking
about their ACT results. Eventually, someone asked me, "Hey,
Derek, what was your score?" I dishonestly and sheepishly said,
"I didn't get mine yet." Unfortunately, I could only say that for
so long. A few days later, that same person, who'd been boasting
about his score for days, asked me again, "Hey, did you get your
score yet?" My off-the-cuff response was, "I got a 25." Yes, I had
felt the need to lie to him again. I mean, everyone else was talking
about their scores of upper 20s and lower 30s.

A couple of months later, I retook the test. Soon afterward, while I was watching a *Saved by the Bell* episode on a Saturday morning, the second round of results arrived. My composite score was 20 out of 36. WHAT?? I was devastated. This time, I actually read the entire report.

I Flunked…Badly

My Mathematics, Science Reasoning, and English scores were all average or above average; however, my Reading score was 11, which was in the bottom 10 percent. Basically, I flunked reading…big time. Below the scoring, the report went on to say, "If you feel your scores are low, don't be discouraged." Yeah right. I felt entirely hopeless.

My high school guidance counselor, Mr. Greg Schmill, knew my pain. Thankfully, he flipped over the results page. On the other side, it read, "Remember that test scores do not guarantee success or failure in college. Other factors count, too." After Mr. Schmill showed me that, I had to ask, "What other factors count?" He told me to think about my positive attitude toward basketball. "Nobody has a better attitude than you. What if you applied that same positive attitude toward college?"

Mr. Schmill was right. Before taking the second ACT test, I had changed nothing, and what was basically my non-effort, clearly showed. To go from where I was to where I wanted to be, I'd have to adopt a positive mindset.

Your Most Basic Need

In order to live, your body's most basic need is water. Similarly, if you want to grow, the most basic prerequisite is a positive attitude. **Your attitude is easy enough to change, and big enough to matter.** According to Martin Seligman, the father of positive psychology, 60 percent of happiness is determined by our genetics and environment, while the other 40 percent is up to us.

Without a positive attitude, you're on the track without a vehicle. When you become positive, you create momentum toward your vision or preferred future. You can't truly *Move to Grow* or make any forward progress in life without accepting full responsibility for your attitude.

Attitude Is *Not* Everything

Attitude is your most basic building block for growth; however, it's important to note that attitude is not everything. Here are a few examples. First, you can have a great attitude but still get fired if you don't perform in key areas. Second, you can have a great attitude but you still won't have more than twenty-four hours in a day. Third, you can have a great attitude, but still not be great at everything. Let's explore this one a bit deeper.

Many people are firm believers that *anyone* can do *anything* that they set their mind to. For instance, take the best basketball player ever, Michael Jordan. If I wanted to play basketball like Michael Jordan, it would never happen. Realistically, even if I practiced basketball for twelve hours a day, seven days a week, 365 days a year (which I pretty much did for a couple years of my life), I would still never be able to play like Michael Jordan. You must have a general awareness of yourself and your capabilities.

One of my most painful memories came when I was a senior basketball player at Wisconsin Lutheran College. During the off-season, I worked harder than anyone. On senior day, which was the last game of my collegiate career, I didn't even get into the game. Unfortunately, not everyone has the ability to do what they would love to do, even if they have the best attitude.

"Too Intangible" and "Too Hard to Measure"

In 2012, I taught APE in a corporate setting for the first time. I vividly remember one person who came up to me afterward and said, "I get the passion and the execution, but I don't buy the attitude...it's just *too intangible*." A couple of weeks later, I facilitated the same workshop, and a participant who was a manager came up to me afterward and said, "I don't teach positive attitude to my team because it's *too hard to measure any change.*"

After the first question, I did nothing. After the second question, I wondered, "Is APE all wrong? Am I confusing people with something that you can't teach? Does my attitude even matter? I say yes, it has to matter. Whenever people see me, they often comment on the power of my positivity. But, if you can't measure attitude, should I stop teaching it? I'm not much of a data person, so how should I respond?" My friend, Dr. Rainer J. Meisterjahn, mental coach and owner of Courtex Performance, reminds me that, "Behavior is a direct reflection of attitude, and, in that sense, is measurable. If I see a basketball player physically hang their head and drop their shoulders fifteen times a game on average during one season, and then only three times a game throughout the next, it's a likely indicator of a positive change in attitude."

Synonyms That Changed My Thinking

It was time for some deep reflection. I blocked off a few hours and started reading over the participant evaluations for those two workshops. One question on the evaluation was, "What one topic would you like to see by Derek or another speaker?" Believe it or not, 25 percent of the audience wanted to learn more about attitude. Of all the topics in the world that they could have selected, one out of four chose attitude.

Google also agrees that attitude is important. In fact, Google has over 300 million links about attitude. After realizing this, I thought to myself, "What does attitude even mean to people? People are probably confused." After doing a fair amount of research, I formally defined attitude as, "a settled way of thinking or feeling, by you, about someone or something."

This definition helped, but it wasn't enough for me because it didn't have enough impact to influence others of the true power of a positive attitude. It just seemed too general, so I paid attention to conversations that I had over the next month. During this time, I wrote down or texted myself all the words or synonyms that people used instead of the word attitude.

After brain dumping the words and synonyms, I cleaned up my list and ended up with a total of seventeen words:

1. Perspective
2. Position
3. Posture
4. Mindset
5. Feeling
6. Outlook
7. Culture
8. Approach
9. Mood
10. Reaction
11. Angle
12. View
13. Stance
14. Twist
15. Opinion
16. Believe
17. Energy

I started to link moments or stories to each. This exercise really helped me clarify just how often and in how many ways we think about attitude without even knowing it. Additionally, it helped me redefine attitude as, "A *mindful* way of thinking or feeling, by you, about someone or something." It is *your* responsibility to pay attention to *your* attitude.

17 Moments to *SHIFT* Your Attitude about Attitude

#1. The Cup of "Joe" that Gave Me PERSPECTIVE

One busy fall afternoon, as I sat doing paperwork at the Wisconsin Athletic Club (WAC), I overheard a club member who was spending time directly outside my office. He was engaging with other members and our employees. At one point, he even peeked into my office to say hello. I looked up and responded, but I kept working on my day-to-day operational tasks.

Thinking for a moment about his extremely high amount of energy and positivity, I couldn't help but get up and introduce myself to him. I learned that his name was Joe Torcivia. After talking with him and getting to know him for a few minutes, I praised his high spirits. He then told me quietly that on February 18, 2012, he had suffered a grand mal seizure. Soon after, he had been diagnosed with stage three astrocytoma, or terminal brain cancer.

His cancer hadn't appeared to stop him in the least. I'll never forget what he said next. "I try to have such a positive attitude and try my hardest to live a stress-free life, because stress can literally kill anyone. None of us knows when we are going to die." (It is well established that stress is the most likely trigger of a recurring grand mal seizure.) Joe went on to say, "I'm ecstatic to be here…I can spend the day in bed recounting the difficulty with my brain, or I can get out of bed and be thankful for the things that work well." Whenever I think about Joe's response, I'm reminded of these words by theologian and author J. Sidlow Baxter: **"What is the difference between an obstacle and an opportunity? Our attitude toward it."**

A month later, I again ran into Joe at the club, during his workout. Coincidentally, that same afternoon, I saw him again at a hospital where I was attending a work meeting. Both times, Joe was living in the moment with high spirits. He was such an inspiration to me that I asked him if he would be interested in speaking to our leadership team about the benefits of choosing a positive attitude. Joe willingly accepted.

A few months later, Joe and I sat down together for a cup of "Joe." I revealed to him what I had been considering for some time, and said, "Joe, I want to hire you. You perfectly embody our mission, vision, and values. Would you be interested?" Joe quickly responded, "Unfortunately, I cannot. My doctor said that working would be too stressful for my condition."

Disappointed, I refused to give up. About a week later, I ran into Joe at the club. This time, I said to him, "Joe, here's our mission card. You see, our mission is that 'we make a difference in people's lives,' and we get to have a lot of fun doing it. We're a team. Do you think your doctor would change his perspective if you showed him what we really do here? Would he or would you still consider it too stressful?"

After hoping and praying that we could help Joe while he helped us, I received the great news. Two weeks later, Joe started working with us, and the rest is history. Joe's doctor had changed his perspective on Joe's stress level. I'm happy to say that Joe continues to live years past his doctor's expectations.

I believe that Joe, his doctor, and I have all grown through our experience together. My buddy Joe would tell you that it's simply a matter of *perspective* that makes the big difference.

STOP **Where in your life might a simple *SHIFT* in PERSPECTIVE possibly make a big difference in your or someone else's life? Write it down…and then make the *SHIFT*.**

_____

_____

_____

_____

_____

#2. Choose Your POSITION:
You Can Moan and Groan, But You Can't Moan and Grow

I'll never forget the time that I attended my first workshop about attitude. The speaker was John C. Maxwell. He started the session by asking everybody to stand up and greet a few people for thirty seconds like they were unimportant or insignificant. Then he asked everybody to greet a few people for thirty seconds like they were your long-lost friends or family members. Maxwell paused and said, "Which one created more energy: option one or option two?" We all yelled, "Option two." Maxwell said, "All you did was change your attitude."

Let's take a moment and reflect on today. This morning, did you bounce out of bed with enthusiasm, or did you splat back to your pillow with regret? American Poet Maya Angelou once said, **"This is a wonderful day. I have never seen this one before."** Assume the best in your day. Assume the best in others. If you assume the best in others, others will assume the best in you…and you will see a significant *SHIFT* in the attitudes all around you.

You get to choose your position: positive or negative, opportunity clock or alarm clock. Just as attitude is a choice, personal growth is a choice. You can moan and groan, but you can't moan and grow. You don't need a degree. You don't need a new job. You don't even need luck. You are in control of your attitude toward growth and already have all the resources that you need. You just need to make a choice.

> You can moan and groan, but you can't moan and grow.

 What POSITION will you choose for your own personal growth? It's a simple choice.

Circle One: Positive   Negative

#3. Look at Your POSTURE in the Mirror

My daughters love my phone. As soon as I put it down, they'll grab it, run away, giggle, and hide. Then, they activate the camera, switch the setting to the selfie view, and take pictures or videos of themselves. They are usually standing tall with great posture, and they're happy and filled with lots of energy.

Unfortunately, our external posture can change as we age, which often leads to pain. Let's take this one step further. Amy Cuddy, Harvard Business School psychologist, coauthored a 2010 study that gave rise to the concept of "power posing," which is adopting and holding certain open and assertive postures as a technique for improving performance. The study revealed that participants who power posed had increases in testosterone, decreases in cortisol (the stress hormone), and increased risk taking in a gambling task, as compared to members of a group who adopted meek postures.

How is your external posture? Does your body language shape who you are?

How is your internal posture? Are you positive or negative, happy or grumpy?

Just as a personal trainer can improve your external posture, I'm your companion for working on your internal posture.

After the crash, my internal posture was terrible. I had to pause to propel. Standing up straight and regaining my external posture was crucial for helping me have a positive attitude and be more confident toward addressing my problem.

STOP **Straighten your POSTURE. Look at yourself in the mirror. (If you don't have a mirror handy, go to the selfie view on your phone.) Write your answer to the following question: what tweak(s) do you have to make to your external posture to positively impact your internal posture?**

_____

_____

_____

_____

_____

#4. It Only Takes a Moment to Change Your MINDSET

In 2001, I started my senior year at Wisconsin Lutheran College. At the same time, I was also blessed to be hired as a video scouting intern for the Milwaukee Bucks. My first assignment was to purge all the VHS tapes from the 1990s to create space for the DVD decade of the 2000s.

While all my friends were telling me how awesome it was that I was working in the NBA, I had days when working in a dark, windowless video storage closet didn't seem all that cool. There were times when I didn't want to go to the airport at midnight in the middle of winter to warm up the vehicles for the players and coaches after their road games. Have you ever had a job like that—one that sounded glamorous to others, but maybe had its not-so-great moments?

During that same year, I was also the vending manager for the Milwaukee Brewers. My main responsibility was to hire the best beer vendors and train them to actively sell and yell, "Beer here!" during the home games at Miller Park. Every week, we had a managers' meeting led by our general manager, Tom Olson.

At one of the meetings, Tom said something that struck me. He passionately stated, "Derek, when I was a porter..." (A porter is someone who physically moves the product from the warehouse to the concession areas.) The beginning of Tom's sentence was all that I remember, but it was incredibly meaningful, given the timing. I immediately told myself that if Tom could enthusiastically start at the bottom and work his way to the top of an organization, then I could, too. To start the journey, something would have to change.

The next day, I was scheduled to sort tapes for the Bucks. When I came into work that day, I had a little more pep to my step...because I arrived with a whole new mindset. I could see more clearly that my current role at the bottom of the totem pole was a necessary step on my way to, hopefully, one day becoming a head coach or general manager. I began to notice that everyone around me, including Bucks' general manager Larry Harris, had started at the bottom, too.

The power to accelerate your growth is right in front of you...if you have a growth mindset. Believe that your most basic abilities can be developed through dedication and hard work. It only takes a moment or a green light to change.

STOP **Do you need to change your MINDSET to a growth mindset? If so, write down the internal changes that you need to make...and then make the necessary changes.**

_____

_____

_____

_____

_____

#5. Are you FEELING that you "have to," or that you "get to" do things?

How often do you wake up and start your day with a list of things that you "have to" do? What if you changed that to a list of things that you "get to" do?

 Take a moment and write down three things that you "get to" do.

1.
2.
3.

There are millions of people who would do anything to have your "get to" list. In fact, your worst day might be someone's dream day…the difference is attitude.

Look back at your "get to" list. Do you feel energized? I do. I get to spend time with my family. I get to exercise. I get to read, write, and speak about personal growth and leadership. When I feel great, I gain momentum to *Move to Grow*.

All our "get to do" lists are different; however, one thing that we all get to do is serve others. **When you serve others, they will *feel* your attitude.** If you want to feel better or help others feel better, give more of yourself.

Think about the different people that you spend your time with over the course of a week. Consider how many lives you positively influence, day in and day out. You give of yourself—of your priceless time and energy, as well as other gifts of value—some material, some intangible. I bet you're feeling energized right now just thinking about being able to make a difference in someone else's life. Did positivity just hit you?

When you give to others, you receive a gift, too: happiness. Knowing this, I started to contemplate some of the ways in which so many different people have given to me and helped me. As I began jotting down examples, I quickly realized that I've been given a plethora of gifts by others!

When I was in preschool and grade school, my mom regularly brought me to the nursing home where she worked. I'm grateful for the nursing home experience. She taught by example how to nurture others.

When I was in high school, my dad attended all my basketball games. My dad gave me the gift of his presence. Not just at my basketball games, but whenever it really mattered to me.

During a long meeting, my wife and daughters stopped by and stuck a Post-It note on my computer monitor at work that said, "We love you and miss you!" My family gives me their love and devotion.

What do others give to you? I've been blessed. You've been blessed. Don't wait until Thanksgiving to say, "Thank you." So yes, *SHIFT*...but be grateful for what you have, too. After all, gratitude is an attitude.

STOP **In the next week, you "get to" make a positive difference in the lives of three people. First, figure out which three people you want to serve this week. Grab a pen and write down their names. Next, jot down what you will actually give to each person. Finally, perform each action and enjoy FEELING on fire with positivity and happiness!**

_____

_____

_____

_____

_____

#6. Don't "Peter Out!" Pay Attention to Your OUTLOOK

Have you ever heard of *The Peter Principle*? If not, it's a book that was first published in 1969. The premise is that, too often, people are promoted past their level of competence, thereby becoming incompetent. Unfortunately, this idea is still very common today.

I have witnessed many instances of people being promoted who were not capable of performing at the higher position. I once promoted a sales superstar to a leadership role. We celebrated and congratulated this person. My expected outcome was that the same, high-level results would occur. Unfortunately, the person "petered out" because it takes an entirely different skillset to sell and motivate yourself vs. inspiring and leading a large team.

In this type of a situation, both parties generally lack the right outlook. The people who get promoted don't take personal responsibility to learn, grow, and develop the new skills they need. Meanwhile, the hiring managers don't paint the picture or provide the right path for the people who want to grow. Thus, the people promoted never reach their full potential necessary for the significantly different role.

STOP **What percentage of your potential are you achieving right now? Do you want to increase that percentage by growing or being promoted? If so, avoid petering out by ensuring that you have the right OUTLOOK. Starting today, write down strategies you can take to develop the skills that you need to truly live up to your potential? For example, could you hire a coach, consume self-help material daily, or take on a challenging project?**

_____

_____

_____

_____

_____

#7. Is Your CULTURE a Panacea or a Poison?

In Wisconsin, we get really excited when spring arrives. We finally get to spend some time outdoors to enjoy the sun and the crisp, fresh air. One year, my spring cleanup was unforgettable, as well as regrettable. I mulched, edged, trimmed, cut, and fertilized the lawn. The last thing that I did was spot-treat the weeds in the lawn, flower beds, and sidewalk cracks.

The next morning, Rachel woke up, opened the blinds, and said to me, "Derek, did you spray the weeds yesterday?" I told her I had, and she went on to say, "Why did you spray the hosta plants? They're definitely not weeds and now they're all dead!" Unfortunately for me, the hosta plants were the first things that you saw when you walked out the back door of our house. Without the thick hosta for cover, you now saw an ugly fence from 1954.

Rachel wasn't very happy, and she had good reason. Regrettably, I had accidentally killed our fence cover. But I was confused, which was not all that uncommon when it came to our horticulture. I never sprayed the hostas directly; rather, I sprayed around the area. The weed killer must have seeped into the cracks of the walk and into the roots of the hosta. That, or it blew on them from the wind. Unfortunately, the poison of the spray wiped out what had been our panacea of fence cover.

A couple of weeks later, after I had gotten over the embarrassment of what had happened, I started to realize that there was a direct correlation between my weed killer/hosta incident and negative/positive people in my life. **People with negative thoughts can become the weed killer to your panacea of good and affirmative thinking and feeling.**

 Take a moment and jot down the names of the six people you spend most of your time with. Try to choose one to two people each from at least three different settings: at home, on a sports team, at work, at a volunteer organization, or anywhere else.

1.
2.
3.
4.
5.
6.

On your list, do you know someone who is poison and complains about everything? I have someone on my list, and unfortunately, I can be that person, too. We all take our turn at being draining or difficult, don't we?

On the other hand, do you have someone on your list who is your panacea, who sees revitalization in everything? I know that I do, and I find myself wanting to spend more time with the people who are happy, positive, and really living life.

Let's go back to your list. On a scale of 1–10, with 1 being a draining person and 10 being an energizing person, place a rating by each person's name. Next, add up all the ratings. Then, divide the total number by 6 to calculate the combined average. Save this number.

Imagine that you asked each person on your list to rate you from 1–10. They would probably rate you the same number that ended up being the combined average from your own list. The attitude and actions of the people around you will influence your own attitude and actions. Emotions are contagious. Debbie Downers influence and create Debbie Downers. Happy Harrys likely create Happy Harrys. I say, spread the cure, not the sickness.

Try to avoid negative people…after you've shown them great compassion. Surround yourself with happy people. Why is this important? According to research by Dr. David McClelland of Harvard University, **your reference group determines as much as 95 percent of your success or failure in life.** According to *The Happiness Advantage* book, **a happy workforce increases productivity by 31 percent, sales by 37 percent, and accuracy by 17 percent.** It's so powerful that it's a wonder why more organizations wouldn't take the time to find out what would make their biggest assets happier at work. One of the best ways to begin is to create a culture of positivity.

 Continually improve the CULTURE around you. Write down ways that you can spend more time with the nines and tens—the people who motivate you—and less time

with the ones and twos—the people who deplete you. For example, take a nine or ten out for lunch every month.

_____

_____

_____

_____

_____

#8. Do You Have an Optimism-First APPROACH?

Just like we learned that you get to define success in your own terms and you get to change your attitude, now you'll learn that you get to choose your approach.

For 365 straight days, my youngest daughter, Mia, wanted to listen to Pharrell Williams' song, "Happy," in the car on the way to school and everywhere else we went. As you can imagine, this was becoming unbearable. Ellie, my older daughter, regularly protested that the song was annoying and gave her a headache…and I was feeling the same way as Ellie. Thankfully, Ellie ultimately said, "Mia, just be happy. You don't need a song to make you happy."

That moment made me think about a keynote that I attended by Bert Jacobs, the founder of Life is Good. During his speech, he repeated, **"Optimism is the most powerful tool for your success. You must be optimistic before you'll have success…not the other way around."** This is so true.

After reflecting on what Bert Jacobs ingrained in my head throughout his talk, I have come to believe that good things happen to me because I remain positive…even in stressful circumstances when it is easy to get upset or to develop a negative attitude. Good things happen in our athletic club because we smile, have fun, and let our personalities shine before we work hard to transform lives. Our approach matters.

Think to yourself for a moment. Do good things happen to you because you have a positive attitude? Or are you a positive person because of the good things that happen to you? Positive people make an effort to be happy and joyful and contented. Don't get caught in the trap of thinking that you're a happy person because good things happen to you. Having a positive attitude is what will produce positive growth.

STOP **The beginning of your day sets the tone for your attitude, so now is the time to change your APPROACH. Write down ways that you can cleanse your attitude daily to flush out your negative thoughts and toxins. For example, meditate for ten minutes every night before you go to bed. Do this consistently and you'll build your attitude in the same way that you would build any muscle.**

_____

_____

_____

_____

_____

#9. Don't Base Your MOOD on an Illusion

I remember it like it was yesterday. Early one morning, I was sitting in the video room working on some clips for our team. Soon after, one of my bosses walked into the practice facility with his head down and didn't say hello to anyone. Have you ever encountered this from a boss?

My immediate reaction to the person next to me was, "I think coach might be mad at me...he seems like he's in a bad mood." Within minutes, a number of my colleagues were saying the same thing throughout our basketball office.

For some reason, when I was working in college and professional basketball, I always worried about how the head coach felt. Looking back, I was wrong in assuming that the head coach was in a bad mood. I simply created the illusion that he was mad at me, without having any knowledge of anything else pertaining to his day. Maybe he just received a call that we had lost a top recruit; his mom or dad may have been ill; his children could have slept poorly; or maybe he had the flu.

Too often we make negative assumptions about other peoples' moods, and these assumptions negatively affect our own moods. Unfortunately, our assumptions are frequently wrong. **You have a choice on what your attitude will be today.** Don't base your mood on an illusion.

STOP **Jot down the name of a boss, colleague, teacher, or "friend" who puts you in a bad MOOD, quite possibly because of your own erroneous assumption. Next, write down an illusion that you are creating. For example, you get irritated when Joe Smith doesn't respond to your email right away. Finally, make the decision to once and for all let go of your assumption. Or, initiate a brutally honest conversation with him or her to hopefully strengthen your relationship and improve the mood.**

_____

_____

_____

_____

_____

#10. Do You Want to "Save Changes" to Your REACTION?

Let's stay at the basketball practice facility for a bit. Only this time, we're moving from the office to the basketball court. There is one practice that I'll never forget, and it came the day after an embarrassing loss.

As you can imagine, the environment was pretty tense. During practice, a coach said to a few of us, "Just get out of my way...

you guys don't do anything in practice anyways…at least clap and have some enthusiasm."

I was crushed. At the time, I didn't know of a better way to handle the situation, so I let my angry emotions get the best of me. Fuming, I excused myself from practice to "use the restroom," but I ended up calling Rachel to vent. After practice, I told everyone in the basketball office what had occurred. At the end of the day, I documented the exact time and place of the incident…to this day, I'm still unsure why. That evening, I called my mom, dad, and close friends. I kept thinking and saying "Did this really happen in front of everyone? I mean…I work so hard. I really need to look for a new job. It's so negative around here. It's not my fault." I truly made the situation that much worse.

It's important to mention that negativity *can* and *will* kill someone's spirit to grow. According to the book, *How Full Is Your Bucket?,* **you should always try to avoid negativity, as it can cut more years off your life than smoking.** Be a bucket filler!

Don't you tire of people blaming other people? Looking back, I realize now that my reaction was wrong. According to Charles Swindol, **"Life is 10 percent what happens to you and 90 percent how you react."** We always taught our players that the person who complained about dropping the ball was usually the one who dropped it most frequently, but I wasn't applying this lesson to myself. During that intense day at practice, I should've shut my mouth and talked to the coach one on one at a later time. **Don't react impulsively. Instead, respond mindfully.**

I see the same overreactions in business and in my personal life. It's hard to grow if you're always reacting negatively and blaming others instead of accepting full responsibility and ownership for everything you experience. After all, you can't blame the dentist if you don't brush your teeth.

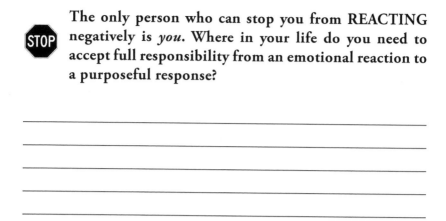

The only person who can stop you from REACTING negatively is *you*. Where in your life do you need to accept full responsibility from an emotional reaction to a purposeful response?

_____

_____

_____

_____

_____

#11. What Is Your ANGLE in Life for Getting Things You Desire?

Do you want more, less, smaller, or bigger? Do you want something entirely different?

 Take a moment and write down three material things that you want.

1.
2.
3.

According to United States census data, the size of the average American home in the 1950s was about 1,000 square feet. Today, the average home is about 2,500 square feet. Houses have ballooned. On top of that, in 1950, 3.37 people lived in each home. Today, only 2.6 people live in each home.

According to a "Life at Home in the Twenty-First Century" UCLA study, 75 percent of families can't park in garages because they are too jammed with things. We also have a $22 billion personal storage industry in America.

According to a Northwestern University study by psychologist Galen Bodenhausen, although American consumer activity has increased substantially since the 1950s, happiness levels have flatlined.

Enough said. Be careful with the "I'll be happy after I get more, more, more" attitude.

STOP **It's easy to have a negative ANGLE, especially about the things that we don't have. Write down three material things that you own, but don't use. Consider donating the items to someone who could truly benefit from having them. Now, jot down three non-material "things" you have that will help you drive toward your vision of fulfillment. Open your eyes both literally and figuratively. You probably have it pretty good!**

_____

_____

_____

_____

_____

#12. Is Your VIEW Crushing Your Dream?

Apart from a lot of basketball games and one season of *The Bachelor*, I've never been into TV. As a kid, I never watched cartoons on Saturday mornings. As for movies, the only ones I remember intently watching were *E.T.*, *Gremlins*, *Home Alone*, *Pistol Pete Maravich*, *Titanic*, and *Super Size Me*.

I have no problem with television or movies. In fact, I wish that I watched more movies. It's rather embarrassing when you're at a table full of people and you're the only one who hasn't watched the movie, *Happy Gilmore*, and it's been the topic of discussion for twenty minutes. When that happens, I disappear for a bathroom break.

Here is where your current view could become a problem for maintaining your positive attitude. According to the Neilsen Media Ratings Company, the average American watches more than five hours of live television every day. This is over one day per week, or over two months per year we spend watching TV. Is TV one of the culprits of you being behind at home and complaining about how busy you are at work?

Do we even need to talk about the time wasted on your phone? According to a Dsout study, **the typical cellphone user touches his or her phone 2,617 times every day**—and that's just the average user. The study found that extreme cellphone users—meaning the top 10 percent—touch their phones more than 5,400 times daily. Is the addiction to your device the big reason that you might not be growing and discovering your passions?

STOP **Do you have enough time to accomplish what you desire? If not, TV time or other screen time just might be the hidden pitfall that is consuming your life, bringing you down, and crushing your dream. Be active and change your VIEW. Starting today, swap 50 percent of your screen time for personal growth time. Write down some different things that you can swap half of your screen time with. For example, read or meditate.**

_____

_____

_____

_____

#13. Is Your STANCE a Part of the Problem or a Part of the Solution?

I'll never forget the time when I was at a water park with my family and a seven-year-old boy asked me what I did for a job. After I told him, he said, "My daddy has a *bad* job because he is a drywaller." Seconds later, his dad looked up and said, "Yep. My job stinks."

It's important that I mention just how tough drywalling is. I helped my dad install drywall when I was younger, and I wouldn't want to do it either. My point, however, is that the boy probably perceived his dad as having a bad job because of his dad's deliberate negative stance. What if the drywaller had responded with something like, "Yep. My job is difficult, and I don't want to do it forever, but right now it provides for our family. I'm grateful to have a job."

As I mentioned earlier, I used to be a complainer. I thought I worked harder than everyone else and was not rewarded for it. I only wish someone had confronted me on my whining earlier to help me see the light. Unfortunately, it wasn't that simple.

I did finally realize it, but it would be years later when my friend, former colleague, and head coach of Pepperdine University men's basketball, Marty Wilson, said to me, **"You're either part of the problem or part of the solution."** My attitude was the problem, and ultimately, I changed my stance by switching careers.

STOP **If you could kick the person most responsible for your problems, you wouldn't be sitting and reading this book. Just think about what would happen if you took a fraction of your negative energy and applied it to becoming a part of the solution. In what area in your life do you want to change your STANCE from being a part of the problem to being a part of the solution? Write it down. For example: you'll stop complaining about busy you are; instead, you'll start asking for help.**

_____

_____

_____

_____

_____

#14. TWIST in the Direction of Truth

Think about the last time you left a job. Did you ever actually know the person who replaced you?

I've been on both sides of this situation a number of times and in all different types of environments. From my own personal experience, as well as from most of my conversations with those who have known their replacements, there seems to be a lot of gossiping about the new replacement. For example, employees and customers have said to me about my replacements, "He's not there as much as you were," or, "She doesn't spend as much time with me as you did."

What I found most interesting is that other people are often gossiping in a similar way to the new replacement about you. For example, employees and customers who are closer to the new replacement than they were to you often say, "You're so much better than her," or "Your staff is so much nicer than his."

After being a part of and listening to countless pity parties, I finally learned that you can change your twist. **You don't have to add fuel to gossip and spread it like wildfire.**

In 2013, I was promoted at the Wisconsin Athletic Club. My superstar replacement, Nikki Wille, was one of my direct reports for a few years prior. The day before our official transition, we made a simple agreement that strengthened both of our businesses. I said to her, "Nikki, people will tell you how great you are and how bad I was. People will tell me how much they miss me and how different we are. Let's always respond to these people about something positive about each other and never give in to their drama. Are you in?"

Thankfully, Nikki was on board. Over the next couple of years, both of our clubs were more profitable and moved in a positive direction. Best of all, we increased our leadership potential as well as our friendship to levels that neither one of us thought were possible. You can spend your time gossiping and kill growth and productivity, or you can spend your time growing and twisting toward the truth.

Do you intentionally or unintentionally gossip and pit people against each other? If so, write down the name of a person whom you wronged. Today, make the decision to TWIST in the direction of truth. Write down one way that you can grow with each other and not gossip about each other.

_____

_____

_____

_____

_____

#15. "Bee" the OPINION of Possibilities

Visualize a swarm of bees for a moment. They all look like they have an intense case of scoliosis, don't they? Bees shouldn't be able to fly, but they do the impossible. To fly, bees must work harder to stretch and flap their wings than most insects.

When I was in college, I played basketball with my friend, David Willems. My mentor, coach Wayne Rasmussen, would always call him *Bumblebee*. David wasn't the most talented or skilled player. Regrettably, some of our teammates, including myself, wondered why he got minutes on the court during actual games.

Coach Rasmussen had the opinion that David was like a bee because he stretched himself and worked extremely hard, especially on defense, to make up for a number of his weaknesses. Coach capitalized on *Bumblebee's* top strengths, which allowed my teammates and me to change our negative opinion or judgment about David's overall skill and talent, to an appreciation for his positive contributions.

Think about an area of your life where you have a negative OPINION or judgment about yourself or someone else. For example, you're frustrated because your family member isn't as organized as you are at home. Write down a way that you can *SHIFT* your negative opinion in this area to a positive, win-win situation, by capitalizing on strengths.

_____

_____

_____

_____

_____

#16. BELIEVE that You Are the Card Dealer

Do you know someone from school who has been extremely successful, but who never would have been considered for valedictorian or magna cum laude? While the details may differ, we all know someone like this. How well you did in school does not always correlate with how well you'll do after school.

The secret is that these people changed their beliefs and attitude about themselves. Move from "These are the cards I was dealt," to "I am the card dealer." Believing in yourself is one of the most important blocks in building your ideal life.

> Move from "These are the cards I was dealt," to "I am the card dealer."

According to a Louisiana State University study, people who believe in themselves use a larger percentage of their brain's cognitive capacity to solve problems. Over time, I changed my belief about myself. There was no way that I was going to let my crash or low ACT scores hinder my growth. My business, Move Results, took five years to develop from its inception to its launch. Five calendar years is a total of 1,825 days. What if I had stopped believing in myself, stopped solving problems, and totally gave up by the 1,824[th] day?

Where will you end up if you give up too soon? It was Dr. Martin Luther King Jr. who said, **"If you can't fly, then run. If you can't run, then walk. If you can't walk, then crawl. But** whatever you do, you have to keep moving forward." See the good in the bad.

STOP **Write down something that you really want to accomplish. To help you power through the tough times, jot down a way that will help you to BELIEVE in yourself more. For example, get comfortable being uncomfortable, talk to people who love you, schedule time to focus, avoid negative self-talk, hire a coach, or be ok with people who don't accept you.**

_____

_____

_____

_____

_____

#17. Take Responsibility for Your ENERGY

On a Wednesday evening, I headed to my daughter's school to pick her up from hip hop class. I arrived a little bit early and decided to join the ever popular "bury your head in your phone" party. A couple minutes later, I looked up when I heard a ton of enthusiasm coming from the gym. I walked over to peek inside and noticed that there was a sign taped on the door that said, "Please take responsibility for the energy you bring to this place." I immediately checked on my own energy level. Before class was dismissed, I quickly snapped a picture of the sign.

> Please take responsibility for the energy you bring to this place.

On our way home, we talked about the class. Ellie said, "Dad, we had so much fun." I said, "The energy sign worked then, didn't it?" Ellie responded, "I guess. I just wish hip hop class was longer, like an hour and a half." I told her I would put on some music so that she could dance in the back seat until we got home. As soon as we pulled into the garage, I turned off the car, the music stopped, and Ellie rather sadly asked, "Are grown-ups too tired to have fun because all they do is work?" Before we walked into the house, I shrugged and said, "Well, it depends." During our ride home, Ellie must have been comparing and contrasting the energy levels of kids and adults. At that moment, our conversation ended, but my mind started to spin.

After the girls went to bed, I couldn't stop thinking about Ellie's question, "Are grown-ups too tired to have fun because all they do is work?" Ellie's question made me think about how many of us go about our days, weeks, months, and years lacking energy and enthusiasm.

A few minutes later, the simple, yet powerful sign that said, "Please take responsibility for the energy you bring to this place," popped back into my head. I wondered, "What if I posted that same sign at work? Would we embrace it or ignore it?"

Do *you* want to be more enthusiastic and energetic? Do you want *your team* to be more enthusiastic and energetic? If so, then act more enthusiastic and energetic. As the sign outside the hip hop class said, "Please take responsibility for the energy you bring to this place." You are responsible for bringing energy and enthusiasm to work every day. Rule yourself!

STOP **Write down three ways that you can bring energy to those environments you spend most of your time in.**

_____

_____

_____

_____

_____

Do You Have the Will to Be More Positive?

According to a *Psychology Today* article titled "Our Brain's Negativity Bias," our brains are more highly attuned to negative news. Because of our negativity bias, we're always going to have negative emotions. In other words, it's impossible to always remain positive. For this reason, **the question is not, "Do you have the ability to be more positive?" The question is, "Do you have the will and desire to work at being more positive?"**

Were You Overwhelmed?

Did the 17 mini exercises seem overwhelming? If so, think of each activity as a small win that is helping you build momentum toward fulfillment. Remember, APE is a marathon, not a sprint. Your regular deposits will pay huge dividends. It is my hope that the moments and action items will help you change your perspective regarding how powerful a positive attitude is with respect to growth and development. Be intentional about having a positive attitude so that your positive emotions outnumber your negative ones. Over time, this mindset *SHIFT* will slowly enhance your progress in just about every area of your life.

Only 12 Inches Connect Your Mind (Attitude) and Your Heart (Passion)

When I was twelve years old, I wanted to be a hunter because a lot of my friends and family hunted. Because of my curiosity and expressed interest, my parents signed me up for a class. This class ended with a skills test. Unlike my ACT test, I passed this one.

Fast forward to today...I've never hunted a day in my life. I ended up not loving it as a kid, and I don't love it now. I learned that you can have the best attitude in the world toward someone or something, but it won't necessarily enhance your life if it isn't one of your passions.

Passion is your fuel for growth. Without passion, you're likely to lose the great attitude and end up with fatigue and burnout. In the next chapter, you'll spend time thinking, dreaming, and personalizing your ambitions. You'll find your X, the intersection where what you love doing (passion) and what you want to be great at (skill) will cross. Unfortunately, many people never experience their X because they've never taken the time to find it, or they don't believe that their dreams can come to fruition. Let's undo most of your negativity once and for all by connecting the 12 inches between your mind/attitude and your heart/passion.

"Attitude" Key Moves

- Take full responsibility for your attitude.
- Create momentum toward your vision with a positive attitude.
- Recognize that optimism comes before success.
- Believe that you can achieve what you desire.

STOP Write down the *first thing* from this chapter's content that you will move to act on.

_____

_____

_____

_____

_____

SHIFT Roadmap: From Attitude to Passions

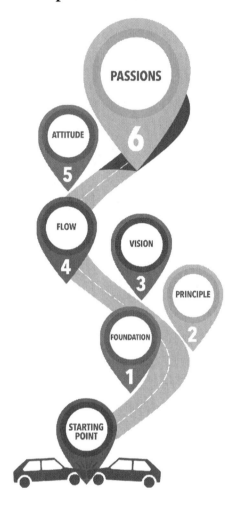

CHAPTER SIX

PASSIONS:
PERSONALIZE YOUR AMBITIONS

"Passion is energy. Feel the power that comes
from focusing on what excites you."

– Oprah Winfrey

T
hink back to when you were in school. If you were like me, you probably stayed up as late as possible playing video games or listening to music. You may or may not have squeezed in a little bit of homework. You were young and invincible, and at night, you never seemed to feel tired.

However, the next morning was a whole different story. In fact, you were toast. I remember those mornings like they were yesterday. Before school, my mom would say, "Derek, get up! Up, up, up!" On road trips, my basketball coaches would pound on the players' doors when it was time to giddy up. If your parents or coaches didn't wake you up completely, you would always hit the snooze button until the very last possible second, to get there just in time.

Vicious or Virtuous Cycle…You Get to Choose

Fast forward to today…Have you changed? Do you bounce out of bed in the morning like an excited kindergartener? Or do you roll over and squeeze in as many ZZZs as you can until you are forced to fall out of bed like a sluggish teenager?

You have a couple of choices. You can choose to loathe life and accomplish next to nothing for twenty-four hours a day. Loathing life becomes a vicious cycle. Or, you can choose to be passionate and productive from the moment you wake up until the moment you go to bed. I call this the virtuous cycle.

I've spent time in both cycles. How about you? Are you in a vicious or virtuous cycle?

Two Questions, One Answer

After a workout at the gym, my friend Ryan Owsianny once asked me, "*How* did you become a morning person?" One week later, at a training session that I was facilitating, a person in the audience asked me, "*Why* did you become a morning person?" Although I never really thought about these questions before, both had exactly the same answer—I finally found my *reasons* to get up. I've become a person with true motivation for making every waking moment count.

Alarm vs. Opportunity Clock

Today, I'm beyond thankful to view my alarm clock as an opportunity clock. I think we can all agree that being alarmed creates negative feelings. Having an opportunity is a positive feeling—one that I want to pursue. Are there days when I feel like sleeping in? Of course there are. We wouldn't be human if we didn't all want to hit snooze on occasion. But here is what I know: **Whatever your reasons are that motivate you to rise early and create a positive feeling, they will always supersede the negative feeling you suffer when your alarm blasts off.**

I haven't hit the snooze button in years. Is it easy every day? No. You can trust me, however, that when you find your reasons, it becomes a lot easier to get out of bed.

You Will Also Find Your Motivation

You might be wondering how I went from being a nighttime procrastinator to a productive morning person. You might wonder what really motivates me. How do I get up with little to no struggle? After a day of pondering this, I realized that I spent an entire year working through key questions to find and clarify my reasons.

If you're struggling through a vicious cycle of getting up every day begrudgingly, don't worry—I used to do the same thing. If you've made it this far in the book, you're about to begin the virtuous cycle of wanting to get up every morning. Soon, you'll be motivated to want to get up because your reasons will be crystal clear.

What are my reasons to get up in the morning? They are simply my passions.

What Is Passion?

Doing what you hate is stress. Doing what you love is passion. Passion is an intense desire or enthusiasm for something. It's what you want to spend your time doing. Passion is not about getting more things. Don't overthink passion. It might be right in front of you.

> Doing what you hate is stress. Doing what you love is passion.

Passions vs. Pleasures

Before starting the process of discovering your passions, it's important to note the difference between passions and pleasures. Passion is long-term desire or enthusiasm, such as relationships, wellness, and personal growth. Pleasure is short-term gratification, such as vacation, wine, and massage. We need both to flourish, but living with long-term passions is more impactful than procrastinating with short-term pleasures.

🛑 Passions Point You Toward Your Vision

Your passions will point you in the direction of your vision. As I mentioned earlier, your vision is your preferred future. Rewrite your personal vision.

Your Vision: _____

Did you already talk yourself out of it, like 90 percent of the population does, because it's too big? Or are you confidently making steady progress toward it? Remember…bit by bit.

There is nothing unrealistic about a vision when it aligns with your passions. Don't dwell on the risk of following your vision—usually, it's not that big of a risk. Stop letting the little voices of doubt get in your way, or simply don't engage those voices. My friend and mental coach, Dr. Rainer J. Meisterjahn says, "We can't directly control the thoughts that pop into our head, but we can make a conscious choice about whether and how to act on them. You don't have to identify with the doubts your brain creates!" By the end of this chapter, you'll have started to cultivate your passions on your foundation…if you keep moving.

Why Are Passions Important?

Your passions are important for many reasons, but there is one reason that is particularly important. When you're passionate about something, you'll have a better chance to grow and reach your potential. **Passions give you the motivation to break through just about any wall.** It's much easier to achieve your goals when it doesn't feel like work. Passion is your fuel and ignition for growth.

Don't be the person who has to wait until the next vacation or retirement to travel or enjoy life. The reality is that vacation time is typically only about 5 percent of one's time. If you're in the middle of your career and already thinking about retirement, you're most likely not enjoying what you do every day. You want to check vacations and retirement off your list, but you don't want to check off passions. The magic happens in your passion zone.

Do You Need a Job with Benefits or Want the Next Job Promotion?

Growing up, I would always hear, "Make sure that you get a job with solid benefits, such as health insurance, 401K, and vacation," and, "What is your next step or job promotion?" To this day, I hear from some of those same people, "Ugh. I cannot wait to get away from work next week and enjoy my vacation." Can you relate?

Over time, however, my perspective has changed. Today, my goal remains to keep growing and to have a job with benefits, but with the benefits that are right for me. Not everyone wants or needs traditional employer benefits or the next job promotion. I've learned that many people prefer to be entrepreneurs and enjoy the benefits of decision-making authority, flexible work schedules, and most importantly, doing what they're passionate about. Move beyond job titles and see the world as your playground. After all...a job promotion is only a step up if you actually *want* to do it.

> A job promotion is only a step up if you actually *want* to do it.

Find Your Fit...It's Your Responsibility

Now that we know how important passions are, it's time to find your fit. What does this mean? Because passions are personal, we all have different ones. Find *your* specific passions or fit, not somebody else's. Let's look health and fitness as an example of how to *SHIFT* one's focus to find one's passion.

Does *Exercise* Have to Be Boring?

We all know how important exercise is, so why don't we commit to it daily? According to the Center for Disease Control and

Prevention, only half of Americans meet the physical activity guidelines for cardio or aerobic activity. According to the International Health, Racquet & Sportsclub Association (IHRSA), fewer than one out of five people belongs to a gym.

The sad reality is that the majority of people despise, or at the very least dislike, exercising. Unfortunately, people who dislike exercise find it to be boring and bothersome, rather than viewing it as a stress-reducing activity. They don't see the benefits of how exercise can clear our minds as well as help to keep us fit and healthy. Non-exercisers, arguably, don't entertain the idea that exercising could actually become something they look forward to doing while having some fun at the same time. If you're one of the few people who belong to a gym and enjoy working out, welcome to the group of crazies. If you're not one of these people, don't worry...there's a solution.

Most people who tell me that they hate to exercise don't actually hate exercise. You certainly can change your mindset and discard any negativity that you associate with working out. Throw out all your preprogrammed notions that tell you that exercise is too hard, too complicated, or too boring. I believe you can have fun exercising by finding your perfect fit. Figure out the physical activity that you enjoy. Find something that makes you want to work hard but also have fun, while reaching your fitness goals. If you don't enjoy exercising, you don't hate exercise; you just haven't found something that you can enjoy doing.

So, after some time, if you find an activity that you enjoy doing, like a dance-type group fitness class, and you reprogram yourself to find value in exercising and getting fit, you'll eventually feel passionate about what you are doing. You'll begin to look forward to your workout time.

Does *Work* Have to Be Boring?

The same journey of finding your exercise niche directly relates to being passionate about your work. We all know how important it is to be passionate at work, so why don't we make the necessary moves to actually be happy at work? According to Gallup, over 70 percent of Americans are disengaged at work. How can we be so busy, yet so bored? Many of us spend 60 to 70 percent of our non-sleeping hours at work. Don't you think loving it should be a priority?

If you want to be engaged, don't wait for your employer to engage you. Do the work in finding your passions. You are responsible. It is vitally important to find your fit at work, just as you find your fit at the gym. Remember, your passions point you in the right direction.

People constantly tell me about things that they should be doing, but aren't, because they hate doing them. They say, "I hate exercising. I hate reading!" I usually ask them, "What kind of exercises are you doing? What are you reading? What are your interests? Have you tried reading about your interests and hobbies? Should you be listening to an audiobook instead? Maybe you hate traditional running on the treadmill, but have you tried swimming for cardio, or playing basketball?" If you find yourself struggling to do certain things, be sure to ask yourself the pertinent questions about why it's a struggle.

The entire time that I was in school, I always hated reading. Heck, I hated reading until I was in my late twenties, and for one simple reason—I wasn't reading the right material.

What things are you deeply passionate about? We'll be going through a number of specific questions to help you find your answers to this question. Once you find your fit, you'll be one of the crazies who is actively engaged in work and life.

🛑 "Love to Do" vs. "Like to Do"

To get your mind thinking in your passion zone, I want you to do a quick brain dump. In the section below, write down seven things that you Like to Do. For example, you might *like* doing business operations, spending time with your friends, or reading a nonfiction book. Then, write three things that you Love to Do. For example, you might *love* driving sales, investing time with your family members, or listening to a fiction audiobook.

I said the word love for a very specific reason. You can *like* doing a lot of things, but you can't *love* doing a lot of things. This will help you find your current location. If you don't know where you are now, even the best map won't help you reach your destination. *Keep in mind that your location is always changing, so don't worry about writing something down that you're not 100 percent sure about.*

Like to Do:

1.
2.
3.
4.
5.
6.
7.

Love to Do:

1.
2.
3.

Do more of what you love and less of what you like. Because you're growing, where you are now is not where you'll be tomorrow.

> Do more of what you love and less of what you like.

Find Your X's—Love It and Be Great at It

Now that we know what passion is, why passions are important, and who is responsible for finding your passions, it's time to find your X's. An X is the intersection of what you love to do (passion) and what you want to be great at doing (skill). See diagram. Skill is the ability to do something well, usually gained through learning or experience. I discovered the X concept after I made the transition from working with basketball players to leading fitness professionals. I realized that I loved *playing* basketball, but I no longer wanted to get better at *coaching* basketball. Today, I love personal growth, and I continually strive to get better at helping others to grow.

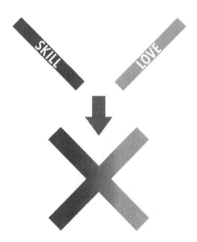

Passion in Action

A successful intersection or a completed X is a passion in action… fulfillment. You need both love (forward slash) and skill (backslash) for an X because you can love what you do and *not* be great at it… frustration. Or, you can be great at what you do and *not* love it… boredom.

Each person can have multiple X's. Three strikes in this situation is a good thing. You want to spend as much time as you can on what you love to do and what you're great at doing.

In this chapter, you'll find your completed X's. *In the next chapter, you'll learn how to be laser-focused on executing your X's. You'll learn how to get better at what you want to be great at.*

/ = Forward Slash of the X: Ten Questions to Help You Find What You Love

Becoming self-aware is one of the most important things you can do to discover your passions. Let's find the first slash of your X's. What is it that you love? If *you* don't know *your* loves, how is anyone else supposed to know them?

To do this, you'll need to intentionally think and direct your mind toward your X's, free of distractions. Reread your Love to Do vs. Like to Do list. Relax and spend as much time as you can to find your X's, or sweet spots. Go to the library or coffee shop and pretend that your phone or laptop died. With just a pen and some paper, answer the following series of questions and capture your thoughts...focus. *I've shared my answers to give you examples. Next to each of my answers, I tagged my passions that came up over and over again in parentheses.*

1. **What are you best in the world at? (Yes, you're best in the world at something.)**
   ○ *I'm best in the world at my commitment to growing. (Personal Growth)*

2. **What gives you the greatest meaning?**
   ○ *Knowing that the people closest to me love me, respect me, and want to be around me, gives me the greatest meaning. (Relationships)*

3. **What do you never want to give up on?**
   ○ *I never want to give up on my family, friends, coworkers, and faith. (Relationships)*

4. **What do you want to be remembered for?**
   ○ *I want to be remembered for moving others to grow. (Personal Growth)*

5. **What do you never want time away from?**
   - *I never want time away from my family. (Relationships)*

6. **What makes you want to get up and move?**
   - *Personal growth and staying active with my family makes me want to get up and move. (Relationships, Wellness, Personal Growth)*

7. **What is your dream?**
   - *My dream is my vision, which is to help move one million people from frustrated to fulfilled. (Relationships, Personal Growth)*

8. **What do other people come to you for?**
   - *Other people come to me to learn how to get unstuck, grow, and take care of themselves while being so busy. (Wellness, Personal Growth)*

9. **What makes you the happiest?**
   - *I'm happiest when I'm with my loved ones, growing, and being active. (Relationships, Wellness, Personal Growth)*

10. **What would you want people to show you appreciation for?**
   - *I want people to appreciate me for helping them to grow in their personal and professional lives. (Personal Growth)*

My Passions

I'll never forget when Rachel and I went in for the ultrasound appointments for our two precious daughters, Ellie and Mia. We had the biggest smiles plastered on our faces when we heard each of their heartbeats for the first time. A strong heartbeat meant healthy growing life. Later, I was reminded of this special time. While I was answering the ten questions, my heartbeat was strongest when I thought about my passions: relationships, wellness, and personal growth. Being mindful of your heartbeat is appropriate when finding your passions.

🛑 Your Passions

Now it's your turn to find out when your heart beats the strongest. What are your life-changing passions? Take a moment and answer the following ten questions.

1. What are you best in the world at? (Yes, you're best in the world at something.)
2. What gives you the greatest meaning?
3. What do you never want to give up on?
4. What do you want to be remembered for?
5. What do you never want time away from?
6. What makes you want to get up and move?
7. What is your dream?
8. What do other people come to you for?
9. What makes you the happiest?
10. What would you want people to show you appreciation for?

If you haven't already, go back and tag your passions to your answers.

Do you see a theme? If not, continue to work through the questions until you do. A theme is important because it will help you recognize what you genuinely love. *Remember, your passions may change as you grow.* When you're ready, write down your passions.

-
-
-
-
-

\ = Backslash of the X: Ten Questions to Help You Find What You Want to Be Great At

Now that you've found the forward slashes, your passions or loves, let's complete your X's by finding the backslashes to officially create the intersections. Remember, passion by itself is not enough. A completed X is passion in action.

With respect to your passions, the following questions will help you find what you want to be great at. The answers to these questions will be more specific priorities or skills. Don't worry if you have some of the same answers as your passions from the previous ten questions. *Please note that you should ask all ten of these questions with each of your passions. For my answers and examples below, I asked each question to myself solely with my "Personal Growth" passion in mind (not "Relationships" or "Wellness").*

1. **What activities do you do that make the time fly?**
   - *Time flies when I'm preparing for speaking or facilitating an event. (Speaking, Facilitating)*

2. **What would you do if you had no fear?**
   - *If I had no fear, I would help move one million people from frustrated to fulfilled. (Writing, Speaking, Facilitating, Coaching)*

3. **What do you want to be continuously learning about?**
   - *I want to be continuously learning about how to be a better speaker, facilitator, and coach. (Speaking, Facilitating, Coaching)*

4. **What do you have a unique perspective on?**
   - *I have a unique perspective when I'm writing and speaking. (Writing, Speaking)*

5. **What work generates energy inside of you?**
   - *Reading, writing, speaking, facilitating, coaching, and sharing all generate energy inside of me. (Learning, Writing, Speaking, Facilitating, Coaching, Sharing)*

6. **What do you consistently do regardless of whether you receive a paycheck for it?**
   - *I consistently write and share what I learn regardless of whether I receive a paycheck or not. (Writing, Sharing)*

7. **What do you never want to retire from?**
   - *I never want to retire from writing, speaking, facilitating, and coaching. (Writing, Speaking, Facilitating, Coaching)*

8. **What do your heroes or role models do?**
   - *My heroes and role models write, speak, and coach. (Writing, Speaking, Coaching)*

9. **What do you do when you're alone?**
   - *When I'm alone, I read and write. (Learning, Writing)*

10. **What do you want to be doing in three to five years?**
    - *I want to continue to improve as a speaker, facilitator, and coach. (Speaking, Facilitating, Coaching)*

My Priorities

Did you see a theme with my passion of personal growth? I saw six priorities over and over again. I want to be great at learning, writing, speaking, facilitating, coaching, and sharing. I refer to them as my priorities because they are more important to me and fulfill me more than other things.

When I answered these questions for my wellness passion, my priorities were sleeping, eating healthy, drinking water, lifting weights, biking, and stretching. My priorities for my relationship passion were spending quality time with my family, friends, coworkers, and faith. For me to be at my best, I have to be doing what I love and what I want to be great at.

🛑 Your Priorities

Now it's your turn to complete an X or series of X's in your life. What powerful activities fulfill you? Take a moment and answer the following ten questions. Remember, don't rush. Ask all ten of these questions with each of your passions in mind. For now, just pick one passion.

1. What activities do you do that make the time fly?
2. What would you do if you had no fear?
3. What do you want to be continuously learning about?
4. What do you have a unique perspective on?
5. What work generates energy inside of you?
6. What do you consistently do regardless of whether you receive a paycheck for it?
7. What do you never want to retire from?
8. What do your heroes or role models do?
9. What do you do when you're alone?
10. What do you want to be doing in three to five years?

Did you see a theme? If not, continue to work through the questions until you do. When you're ready, write down the priorities or skills that you want to be great at.

-
-
-
-
-
-

When Do You Just Know?

You might be thinking, "When do you just know that you've found an X?" I believe there are two ways that you know: *they* feel your X and *you* feel your X.

They Feel Your X

One day I was having a conversation with my basketball friend and coworker, Mike Mitchell. At work, he stopped by my office after my speaking gig and said, "You have a gift and you're running with it." Mike felt my completed X, or passion, of personal growth and speaking in action.

A couple of months after I started blogging, I walked into an event that was about to start, and some of the people in attendance said, "Your article was exactly what I needed today. The fact that you love what you do really shines through." These people felt my X of personal growth and writing.

A year after I started doing some corporate leadership facilitation, I was asked to do a demo for a company that was interested in hiring me. Afterward, one of the participants said, "You're the best leadership facilitator I've seen at your age." This participant felt my X of personal growth and facilitating.

You Feel Your X

Do *you* feel your fuel or passion burning? Do you feel an element of *play* in your work? The decision I made at age twenty-eight to commit to personal growth was life-changing. It's hard to explain. Today, my passions and skills match my life goals. I'm just an average person with a deep passion and an above-average desire to grow. I feel energized by my X of personal growth and learning, writing, speaking, facilitating, coaching, and sharing.

The people who feel their X get more accomplished, work more, and avoid burnout because they live in their passions and spend time in their strength-zones as much as they possibly can. Let me share a couple of stories.

Never Work a Day in Your Life

On a beautiful summer day, I went for a walk around the neighborhood and I ran into a friendly guy who stopped me to talk. He told me a story of how he crafted and carved wooden prosthetic legs for forty years of his life. He said he never worked a day in his life because he always saw the result of people being able to walk and play sports every day. He felt his X of sports and carving.

Would You Go the Distance for Your X?

In the middle of one of the coldest and most miserable Wisconsin winters that I can recall, my friend and colleague, Deb Shook, was driving to the athletic club at 2:30 a.m. to open the facility. Suddenly, her tire blew out two miles from the club on an icy road. The temperature was roughly 30 degrees below zero with the wind chill. What did Deb do? She didn't call or text anyone. Instead, she decided to walk to the club to ensure that it opened at 4:00 a.m. Deb truly went the distance for her X. She felt her X of wellness and making a difference in people's lives.

What If You Still Don't Know?

Are you *still* unsure of your passions? Do you *still* feel stuck? If so, don't get discouraged. You're in the majority, but you'll soon be in the minority. Remember, I was stuck, too. Early in my career, I wanted to regularly miss work. I was burned out because I hated my job, not because I was working too much. This changed when I finally realized that *I* owned my future, not some organization.

The Accidental Passion

Think back to flow and process for a moment. Do you recall that knowing your passions doesn't always come before spending time on your passions? In other words, some people have to follow their cues, crashes, and opportunities, not their passions. This was me. Experimenting and trying different things led me to discover my passion of personal development. I moved toward learning, after which speaking, facilitating, writing, coaching, and sharing moved toward me.

Is there something that you've been waiting to try? Or, are you too busy to experiment? Contrary to popular belief, being busy can be a positive thing. I'm not saying that you should be rushing around like crazy from appointment to appointment, but maybe you should be busy because you are trying something new. Stepping outside of your comfort zone might create the extreme breakthrough that you've been craving.

Doesn't trying something new to figure out what it is that you truly love sound like a great use of your time? Trust me, going to work and putting in long hours will become less taxing... *if* you put in the time and effort to find your fit.

If You Don't Feel Like It, Move On

It's also important for you to know when the time is right to move on to something else. Do you often say, "I don't feel like it?" One of my first summer jobs was at a factory. Most employees' shifts ended at 3:00 p.m. I vividly remember those same people lining up at the punch clock around 2:50 p.m. every day. They didn't feel like working any longer and were ready to get out of there.

Fast forward to my first job in a corporate America high-rise building...same result. Most employees stopped cold turkey at 5:00 p.m. By 5:01 p.m., they were tripping on each other to get out, only to wait in a line of cars in the parking structure until 5:15 p.m.

Do you want to continue to race to escape your life? Or do you want to relax and explore your passions?

"Is What You Wanted to Be as a Kid Different from What You Want to Be Now?"

When Ellie was in second grade and we were on our way to school, she said, "Dad, turn down the music." After I did so, she looked out the window and asked me, "Is what you wanted to be as a kid different from what you want to be now?" While we didn't have time to go into tremendous detail, I simply responded, "Great question, Ellie. Yes. The key is to find what you love to do and spend as much time as you can doing it." Your passions will change.

What a Difference One Year Makes

Whatever your passions are now isn't necessarily what they'll always be. My most vivid example of my passions changing came early in my career. In 2007, Rachel and I were living with our dog in a new state while I was the director of player development for the University of Utah men's basketball team. One year later... in 2008, Rachel and I were back in Wisconsin, we had our first daughter, we bought our first house, and I was the general manager of an athletic club. Discovering and pursuing new passions is a part of life.

Will Your Passions Conflict?

When you find your passions, everything will become clearer and easier overall. At times, however, they'll be in conflict.

A few months after I nailed down my true passions, I was on a roll with personal growth. Relationships, on the other hand, were a different story. As I was checking my phone every two minutes at home, Rachel said to me, "I feel like we're your lowest priority." To this day, I'm ashamed to have no idea what was going on at home or at work before or after that moment, but I definitely heard what she said. Although I hate to admit it, she was right. In my mind, my relationships were important to me. My actions of actually being present and spending time with my family, however, didn't reflect that reality. My passions of personal growth and relationships were in conflict.

His Love Trumped My Like

When I was a kid, my Grandpa Gates regularly took me fishing. In 1999, he gifted me a fishing trip to Canada for my high school graduation gift. As a teenager, I had no major responsibilities, so it was easy to get up and go. Ever since that trip, my grandpa and I talked about going again. Finally, in 2016, when grandpa was eighty-two years old, we did it. Why did it take so long to go again? I was in a different spot in my life. I had a young family, a demanding day job, and was writing *SHIFT*. You see, I like fishing, but I don't love it. Again, my passions of personal growth and relationships were in conflict. In this situation, I committed to fishing out of love for my grandpa. I'll be forever grateful that we enjoyed another week together.

Who Wins?

One morning at 3:57 a.m., when Ellie was six and Mia was three, they bounced out of bed and ran into our bedroom to wake me up. They shouted, "Daddy, do you want to play?" I responded, "No! Go back to bed. It's pitch dark outside and it's not even 4:00 in the morning yet." Disappointed, they walked with their heads down to their playroom by themselves. I wanted to sleep. They wanted to spend time with me. Looking back, I wish that I would've enjoyed that morning with daughters. My passions of wellness and relationships were in conflict.

When my passions conflict, the "winning passion" varies because every situation is unique. I've finally learned that the key to managing conflicts with multiple passions is to spend time reflecting or discussing your challenges with your loved ones before, during, and after your commitments. Keep the dialogue open!

There Are No Rules

Someone once asked me, "Are you trying to be a speaker or a manager of an athletic club? You can't do both." I've come to the realization that it *is* both. Ideally, I'm leading the gym while speaking a few times per month. If I were only a speaker, I would be on the road and away from my family too much. All this work wouldn't be worth it if my kids didn't remember me as an active part of their childhood. If I were only an athletic club manager, I'd only be living part of my passions. **Don't be limit*ed* by the limit*ing* thoughts of others.**

"You Don't Have to Do What You Love, Do You?"

When Ellie was seven years old, I asked her, "Do you want to be on a soccer team? You love playing it with me in the backyard." She responded by saying, "You don't *have to* do what you love, do you?" Out of the mouths of babes, Ellie already understood that you can do some things just for fun. You don't have to be on a serious team just because you love a sport. You don't have to be paid for your passion. My friend, Jonnie Bock, is paid to be a doctor, and yet he loves to sing and play the guitar for fun. You can choose passion *or* money; you can choose passion *and* money. Just be you. There are no rules.

Passions Are Just the Beginning

Passions are huge. People with passions are more likely to have positive attitudes and are more willing to take risks. Do everything with passion! I strive to grow with passion, workout with passion, love my family with passion, read to my kids with passion, develop others with passion, and go to work with passion. Finding your passions, motivations, and priorities is just the beginning. You still have to actually devote real time and energy to what matters the most to you.

The Intersection of Thinking and Doing

Carefully look over all passions and priorities on your lists. Ask yourself, "Will I commit to action?" You'll only get a Return On

Passion if you execute. Remember, a completed X is passion in action. It's the intersection of just the right amount of thinking and doing. There is a big difference between the two. You've done enough thinking. The way to get started is to stop thinking and start doing. Let's start moving from desire to action. Warning: this movement in your life may result in extreme personal growth and happiness.

Bridging the Gap

Now that you've personalized your passions, it's time to bridge the gap between knowing your X's and living your X's. Passion without execution is pretending. Execution without passion is wasting. Passion *with* execution will transform your life. In

> Passion without execution is pretending. Execution without passion is wasting. Passion *with* execution will transform your life.

the next chapter, you'll put your pedal to the metal and design every minute of your life's activities around your passions and priorities with ten gap-closing behaviors. You'll continue to go from, "I'm so frustrated and busy," to, "I'm fulfilled and living my ideal life right now."

Keep moving. Your life is changing with each word you read and every page you turn.

"Passions" Key Moves

- 🔑 Think about your reasons and motivations for waking up in the morning.
- 🔑 Take responsibility to find your fit...there are no rules.
- 🔑 Answer the questions to determine your X's.
- 🔑 Do more of what you love and less of what you like.
- 🔑 Live your life with passion!

Remember…to receive a one-page summary of *SHIFT*, please visit **DerekDeprey.com/ShiftBookResources** for your complimentary download.

STOP Write down the *first thing* from this chapter's content that you will move to act on.

_____

_____

_____

_____

_____

SHIFT Roadmap: From Passions to Execution

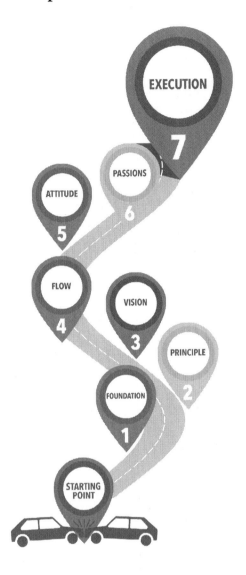

CHAPTER SEVEN
EXECUTION:
EXERCISE MEANINGFUL ACTION

"I tell the players that they can't relive any day in their lives and that they can't relive the minutes of a game, so they should make a great effort, a Mount Everest-type effort, to live up to their potential."

– Al McGuire

In March 2009, I attended the International Health Racquet & Sportsclub Association (IHRSA) convention in San Diego, California. At the event, there was a huge tradeshow as well as hundreds of breakout educational seminars. To get each day started, there was a keynote speaker. Every one of them had published a book or a series of books. I walked away so energized, and I couldn't wait until the next year to go again.

The Moment I Wanted to Write a Book

For the next two years, I attended the same convention. After every keynote, I purchased the speaker's book. I was impacted so positively that I wanted to write my own book and do the same for others. In 2011, as soon as I got on the flight back to Milwaukee, Wisconsin, I started to capture my own quotes, stories, and images to get started. After a couple months, I felt like I was in a groove. I set a deadline to complete the book by April 14, 2013, which would have been my thirty-third birthday. When the date quickly arrived, I had a bunch of categories with bullet points, but no book. I didn't even have a solid working outline. Strike one! I started to talk myself out of my goal.

I Kept Swinging and Missing

A few months later, I decided to hire a ghostwriter to help. Our goal was to complete the book by April 14, 2014. Strike two! Unfortunately, our schedules didn't mesh, and we mutually parted ways. The next year, I hired a second ghostwriter. Our goal was to complete the book by April 14, 2015. Strike three! We also parted ways. The next year, I hired a third ghostwriter. Our goal was to complete the book by April 14, 2016. Strike four! Thankfully, **there's no set number of strikes before you're out in the game of life.**

Was I Insane?

I was doing the same thing repeatedly and expecting a different result. If I were really going to be serious about writing a book, I needed a new way to execute. So, I hired a coach who believed in me, Kary Oberbrunner. It finally hit me that no one could write my book with my authentic stories and moments, but MMI: Me, Myself, and I.

We're all good at talking about what we're going to do. "I'm going to start eating better next week." "As soon as I make more money, I'm going to save money." Is that you? We typically entertain good intentions and have solid plans to move forward, yet too often our lack of execution holds us back from achieving our dreams.

Passions Help You Start and Execution Helps You Finish

Now that you've determined your attitude, discovered your passions, and aligned your passions with your personal vision and values, you can decide what you want to do. Let's move from feeling motivated to actually doing something about it. Having a positive attitude and prioritizing your passions isn't enough. Your passions are simply what matters to you. They help you get started. Your execution is designing your life around what matters to you. It drives you to the finish line.

> Your execution is designing your life around what matters to you. It drives you to the finish line.

To some of you, attitude and passion might seem like common sense. Execution is a choice that might not come so naturally to you. The people who grow and strive to reach their potential take full responsibility for their lives. **Execution is about taking common sense and putting it into consistent practice.** We explored your passions first because they'll help fuel your execution when you hit a wall. Execution of your passions can change your life, but not without effort. Now is the perfect time to *SHIFT* into high gear.

A Plan for Personal Growth

Remember my interview at the Wisconsin Athletic Club (WAC) for a general manager position in 2008? I was asked, "Do you have a plan for personal growth?" I started with nothing. Today, my routine is much more calculated and rigorous than ever. I'm going to walk you through my plan for personal growth. These are the top ten conscious behaviors that I've learned from my own experience, which will help to bring your plan to life. They are my best habits that I've implemented and systematized. Each of these behaviors became vividly clear to me when I started making major progress, mostly as an author and a speaker.

It's important to know two things. First, there is no linear path or exact number of steps required for the behaviors. They can be performed in any order at any time. Second, there is always more than one way for you to execute. **Just like your definition of success and your passions must be personalized, your execution must be personalized as well.** Each of your X's might need different behaviors.

You might only use a few of these ten behaviors, or you may choose to use them all. *Your* plan is the one that will work best for you.

Move from Frustrated to Fulfilled

Before we dive in, think about your personal vision, your passions, and your priorities that you've identified to this point. Now, I want you to look again at your vision of the preferred future that you want to work toward. Based on what you've learned thus far, take a moment and make any necessary tweaks. Once you've decided what it will be, write your vision in the "To Fulfilled" circle of the "*Move to Grow* in Action" diagram. Then, with respect to your vision of the future, write where you are right now in the "From Frustrated" circle. For now, leave the arrow blank. *I've shared my personal example.*

Move to Grow in Action – Derek

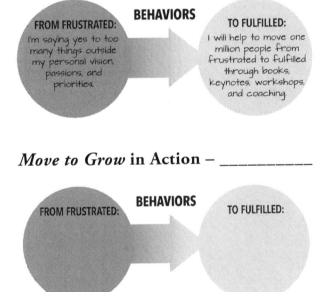

Move to Grow in Action – _____

Ten Behaviors to Execute Your Vision and X's

Throughout the rest of this chapter, think about what behaviors or habits will help you to achieve your vision for the future. What will *your* plan for personal growth be? What will you *put*, and more importantly, *do*, in the arrow?

Behavior #1: Do It Afraid

After I graduated from high school, I had no clue what degree to study for or what I wanted to do for a living. Does this resonate with you? All I wanted to do was play basketball. So, I stayed in my hometown for the first two years of college and attended the University of Wisconsin–Manitowoc. In 1999–2000, during my sophomore year, I met some lifelong friends. We won over half of our games, I scored a lot of points, and I was named to both the First Team All-Conference and All-State teams.

Was I Crazy?

I had a great idea after our last game—an idea that just about everyone else thought was crazy. I wanted to try out for the Wisconsin Badgers, who competed in the prominent Big 10 Conference and had just come off their first Final Four run since 1941. People would say to me, "How do you expect to go from playing at one of the smallest colleges to one of the biggest? You're ridiculous."

The next day, I jumped on our dial-up internet and searched for the address of the Kohl Center, which is where the Badgers practice and play. I handwrote and mailed a letter to the head coach, Dick Bennett, requesting a tryout for his team. Within a week, he sent the following letter to my house...

> *Dear Derek,*
> *I'd be happy to speak with you regarding trying out for our team. We carry 13 people on scholarship and 2 more as walk-on players. They have full benefits except for the scholarship. Next*

season, our two walk-on players will be guards. We're looking for prospects. Sounds like you could be one! Call me or an assistant and we can talk.

Sincerely,
Coach Dick Bennett

I Couldn't Have Imagined a Better Start

Within one week, I received a follow-up voicemail from Tony Bennett, Dick's son and assistant coach at the time. Tony invited me for a two-day summer tryout. Within the first five minutes of the tryout, I made two three-point shots. Hoping to impress, I couldn't have imagined a better start. My heart was pumping with excitement. Unfortunately, big dreams and the best-laid plans don't always come to fruition. I don't remember scoring another basket for the next forty-eight hours. The week after the tryout, I received another letter in the mail…

Derek,

Thanks for attending the tryout. Unfortunately, we're not going to be taking any more walk-ons as we've guaranteed all the spots out. It was a tough decision for us not to take you. I hope you understand. We're most likely filling Julian Swartz's spot with a scholarship player in your spot for this coming fall. I do hope you at least enjoyed your time here. All the best!

Coach Tony Bennett

Reality Check

Fast forward one year…I ended up attending Wisconsin Lutheran College. During my junior year, I quickly realized that I wasn't going to make a living playing basketball. What I did learn, however, was that I could make a living in basketball operations doing video scouting or coaching. One year later, my dream changed, and I really wanted to work in the NBA with the Milwaukee Bucks because of the passion and energy that head coach George Karl brought to the organization. Once again, I was surrounded by doubters. I'd hear things like, "There's no way that you'll be able to work in the NBA if you're not a former player." That may have made me even more determined, because once again, I tried the "letter thing." Only this time, I was looking for a career. Here was my first response from the Bucks in August, 2001...

> *Dear Derek:*
>
> *Thank you for your interest in the Milwaukee Bucks. Unfortunately, at this time we do not have any openings. We will keep your information on file. Best wishes in your employment pursuit.*
>
> *Sincerely,*
> *Ernie Grunfeld, General Manager*

I Kept Trying

I had received a standard dismissal letter. Still, I didn't give up. I received the following letter about three years later...

> *Derek,*
>
> *Enclosed is your 2004 Milwaukee Bucks NBA playoff bonus. Your hard work and commitment in our video department during the regular season and playoffs is very much appreciated. Thank you for your efforts, past and future!*
>
> *Senator Kohl, Owner, and Larry Harris, General Manager*

Do It Afraid

We're all afraid to fail, but we always fail at 100 percent of the things that we don't try. I was terrified to reach out to the Badgers and to the Bucks because most of the people around me said that I was crazy. Also, if you try something and you do fail, that memory may haunt you for a long time. Sometimes, the embarrassing memory is so painful that it can cause you to give up on your dream forever. You give up so you don't risk experiencing that feeling again. Can you relate?

> We're all afraid to fail, but we always fail at 100 percent of the things that we don't try.

As difficult as it was to be rejected by the Badgers, I had to brush off the embarrassment and get right back up and try something else. I gave it another shot and ended up one for two. **Would you be ok with going one for two with some of your biggest fears?** If you want to grow, you have to move out of your comfort zone. Sometimes you just might have to look stupid. Hit the road running and do it afraid. So what if you fail?

STOP **Starting with your vision, write down the top priorities that you want to improve upon or accomplish on the blank lines below. Then, on a scale of 1–10 (1 = low, 10 = high), rate yourself on how committed you are to each of them right now. Circle your numbers. For those of you who don't rate them as 10s, ask yourself what it will take for you to go from the numbers you chose all the way to a 10. Contemplate the obstacles that are holding you back. For example, you want to lose fifteen pounds, but you're a people pleaser and don't block off time to take care of yourself. On the lines below the ratings, write down what's getting in the way of each priority. Now, think about how you can make small moves to overcome and conquer those obstacles. Finally, take the leap and do it afraid for each one!**

Priority #1 _____ (Your Vision)

   1   2   3   4   5   6   7   8   9   10

What's getting in the way of a 10? _____

Priority #2 _____

   1   2   3   4   5   6   7   8   9   10

What's getting in the way of a 10? _____

Priority #3 _____

1   2   3   4   5   6   7   8   9   10

What's getting in the way of a 10? _____

Behavior #2: Set a Deadline

People often ask me, "How do you measure execution?" I typically respond with two questions: "What are you trying to accomplish?" and, "Will you complete it on time?" Now that you've decided what you are trying to accomplish and know that you'll have to do it afraid, it's time to do it...on time.

When I eventually came to the realization that I wanted to become a speaker, I subscribed to speaking blogs, magazines, and books. I studied other speakers at conferences and took precise notes on their delivery. I listened to podcasts and watched online videos. Nevertheless, learning about speaking would only take me so far.

Just Commit

One of the most important things I did was set a deadline to perform my first speaking gig. This was important because it meant that I truly committed to speaking in front of a live audience... afraid. How did it happen? Remember my cues? In 2009, the owners of the athletic club were looking for a speaker to lead a key section of the new-hire orientation. With false confidence on the outside and enormous anxiety on the inside, I raised my hand and said, "I'll do it."

The next day, I went to **FutureMe.org**. Through this website, you can send accountability emails to yourself into the future. In this situation, I set up a series of progress emails to be sent *from* me, and then *to* me. On June 1, 2009, the email that I sent and received said, "Complete orientation outline." On July 1, "Insert personal stories." On August 1, "Complete slideshow and practice in actual room." On August 27, which was the morning after I led the new-hire orientation for the first time, "Congratulations, you're a speaker!" It sure felt good to receive the last one.

Create Momentum toward Achieving Your Vision

Deadlines can be difficult and demanding. However, I know that if I don't set deadlines for myself, I'll find myself too busy or too tired, or I'll question my ability to achieve my goals. Knowing that I had to give a speech on a certain date, I was determined to never miss a day of practice.

Was I perfect? No way! In fact, I was a horrible, nervous wreck. I was sweating profusely and I forgot what I was going to say a few times. Had I failed? Maybe. Had I started to move in the direction I wanted to go, creating some momentum for myself to look ahead and keep my vision in mind? Yes, but I had to learn to be patient. I kept telling myself, "You're twenty-nine years old, but you're only one day into public speaking. You just started." Self-affirmations helped me not to feel discouraged.

STOP Use pressure and stress in a good way to draw out your best performance and potential. Set a deadline or a series of deadlines for your vision (or for each of your top priorities from the last section). Then, go back to the "fulfilled" circle of your "Move to Grow" in Action" diagram. Add the expected deadline. Enjoy the progression toward your wants and aspirations!

Behavior #3: Commit to Daily YOUzones

Now that you understand the importance of setting a deadline, it's important to devote the necessary time so that you actually achieve what you desire. This is where my secret weapon comes into play, which is the YOUzone. **The YOUzone is an intentional daily routine in which you invest "alone time" with no**

interruptions to work on executing your vision, passions, and priorities. The YOUzone can be work or personal time.

How do you focus? Are you ok with being alone? The YOUzone is all about YOU. During this time, you don't schedule team meetings, make phone calls, hit the snooze button, watch TV, or browse the internet. Instead, you wake up in charge of your day and ready to change the world.

Eight Days a Week

Trust me. The YOUzone is a growth accelerator like no other, but only if you consistently hold yourself accountable to getting in the zone. I once had an opportunity to interview with Miami Heat head coach Erik Spoelstra for a video scouting position. At the end of the interview, I asked him, "What habit makes you successful?" He said, "By waking up before the rest of the world, I'm more productive. It's like I get eight days a week." Years later, I ran into him during his pregame workout routine at the athletic club. I thanked him for sharing his habit for success with me, because it has helped transform my life.

Wouldn't you love to have an extra day every week? When you commit to YOUzones, you'll feel like you're getting eight days' worth of work done in one week. You'll wonder how you ever lived without this powerful tool. As you learn about my YOUzone, think about what type of routine will work best for you.

> When you commit to YOUzones, you'll feel like you're getting eight days' worth of work done in one week.

5X More Productive in "Flow"

Before I breakdown my YOUzone itinerary, it's important that I introduce "flow." Psychologist Mihaly Csikszentmihalyi coined the term and defined it as a peak state of consciousness where we feel our best and perform our best. During every YOUzone, you'll spend time in flow. Why is this important? According to

"Is the Secret to Ultimate Human Performance the F-Word?" by author Steven Kotler in *Forbes Magazine*, a ten-year McKinsey& Company study revealed that top executives reported being five times more productive in flow. That means **if you spend Monday in flow, you can take the rest of the week off and still get more done than your steady-state peers.** Let me show you how to get into flow...

My 120-Minute YOUzone Itinerary

5:00 a.m. – Rise and Shine

At 5:00 a.m., I wake up, get dressed, brush my teeth, and guzzle sixteen ounces of water.

No matter what time you go to bed or when you wake up, you have no control over what your bed head looks like, how many pillow lines you have on your face, how puffy your eyes are, or how many times your ankles and knees crack as you get up. You do, however, have a choice as to what time you'll rise. If you're an early bird, you might be annoyingly happy and ready to rock and roll at 5 a.m. If you're a night owl, you might start at 10 a.m. every day. **No matter what your start time is, you have another choice...start your day on fire, or start it with regret.** Think about *when* you're the most productive. Are you most productive in the morning, afternoon, or evening?

5:15 a.m. – Drive to the Coffee Shop and Set Up

At 5:15 a.m., I head to a coffee shop.

The right environment is vital. I love the white noise and people hard at work buzzing around me at coffee shops. No one can stop me with my laptop, Wi-Fi, 80s, 90s, or country music mixes, and a medium roast cup of java. Waking up to this daily pleasure helps me maintain YOUzone consistency. Think about *where* you're the most productive. Aren't you more productive when your environment is just right?

5:30 a.m. – Do Quick Tasks

At 5:30 a.m., I start to feel like I'm accomplishing something by performing my quick tasks list.

Crossing off some undemanding items gets me motivated for what's coming next...a big project. Here are some of my quick tasks: read a devotion, check emails, jot down blog ideas, send birthday and other congratulatory wishes via social media, write a handwritten note, read a few self-help articles and quotes, post the self-help article or quote that provides the most value, and write my agenda for the next day.

6:00 a.m. – Eat the Banana

At 6:00 a.m., I "Eat the Banana," not the frog.

Mark Twain once said, "If you eat a frog first thing in the morning, that will probably be the worst thing you do all day." I believe the opposite to be true, so I changed it to, "Eat the banana," because I'd rather eat a banana than a frog. Let me explain...

If a frog is the worst thing, or something you hate, could a banana be the best thing, or something you love? **You won't want to rise early long-term to taste the dreaded frog.** During this laser-focused 60-minute session, I conquer the biggest project that epitomizes my passions so that I actually want to do it over and over again. Be someone who hungers to wake up for something that you feel passionate about. Eat the banana.

7:00 a.m. – Drive Home and Get Ready for the Day

At 7:00 a.m., I head back home...on fire!

You know that feeling you have after a workout...the endorphins? I have that same feeling after my 120-minute YOUzone. Do I always get everything done that I had planned to do? No. Too often I overestimate what I can accomplish in 120 minutes.

After I get home, I eat breakfast, get ready for work, drive Ellie and Mia to school, and then enjoy my day job.

Does Your YOUzone Have to Be in the Morning?

No. Waking up at 5:00 a.m. doesn't make you successful. It works for me because it's before my family is awake, it's when my brainpower is strongest, and it's usually before I start getting new texts, calls, and emails.

At the athletic club, we have a number of fitness professionals who train clients all morning long. It's their money-making time. The YOUzone for these employees might be best in the middle of the afternoon when the clients are at work and the athletic club schedule is calm. What time will work best for you?

Do I Ever Cancel My YOUzone?

Yes. Although the YOUzone deserves full focus and commitment, there are some things that will trump the YOUzone. Let me share a few examples. First, when my day is booked solid with a bunch of sit-down meetings, I'll replace my YOUzone with an early morning workout. Second, if I have a planned evening engagement, I'll try to stay home in the morning to spend some extra time with my family. Third, during one of my YOUzones, a coworker sent me a text about having knowledge regarding a client being physically abused. The person needed help. Immediately, I stopped my YOUzone and made a phone call. Occasionally, it's ok to cancel.

Am I Too Structured?

Every week, I hear at least one of the following: "You're crazy," "You're over the top," "Anyone who gets up at 5:00 a.m. to get everything done is insane," or, "You're way too structured!" Am I too structured? Maybe I am. But here's what I know…**being structured and disciplined with good habits is better than lacking structure and discipline because of bad habits.** If you're consistent, one day you'll end up with 10,000 YOUzone hours. What could you accomplish if you committed to a YOUzone?

"People Who Do the 10,000-Hour Rule Don't Count the 10,000 Hours."

In the book *Outliers* by Malcolm Gladwell, he teaches the 10,000-Hour Rule. According to Gladwell, the 10,000-Hour Rule is practicing a skill the correct way for about 10,000 hours to achieve world-class expertise. He said, "10,000 hours is the magic number of greatness."

A few years after I learned about the 10,000-Hour Rule, my friend and mentor Mike Bartel once told me, "People who do the 10,000-Hour Rule don't count the 10,000 hours." He was right. Because I got hooked on personal growth and continue to love it, I've written a book and created a motivational speaking and leadership training business…as a result of being focused for 120 minutes per day for five straight years.

> People who do the 10,000-Hour Rule don't count the 10,000 hours.

🛑 Your YOUzone Itinerary

Take a moment and think about how your life would be positively impacted if you committed to daily YOUzones. With respect to your vision, passions, priorities, and deadlines, write your initial YOUzone itinerary. What you write is not set in stone and can be tweaked at any time.

You don't have to fill out all the activities. As you begin, it might be best to focus on one activity, "Eat the Banana." Daily consistency is more important than total length of time spent. Consider starting with fifteen to thirty-minute timeslots or 1 to 2 percent of each day. You can always add more activities and time when you're ready.

YOUzone Date: _____ Time Slot: _____ Location: _____

Activity A: _____ for _____ minutes
Activity B: _____ for _____ minutes
Activity C: _____ for _____ minutes
Activity D: _____ for _____ minutes
Activity E: _____ for _____ minutes

What Will Your Results Be?

I don't know for sure what your results will be, but I would be willing to bet that you'll feel more accomplished and fulfilled. You'll be more efficient and effective. For me, I'm not even close to this 10,000+ hour journey, but I'm already happier, healthier, and wealthier. If you first focus on what you do daily, you will eventually reap the benefits of what you will accomplish annually. Consistent, daily YOUzones multiplied over time will equal long-term growth and results for you, too.

> If you first focus on what you do daily, you will eventually reap the benefits of what you will accomplish annually.

Control Your Discretionary Effort

To get results, you'll find yourself working harder than 90 percent of the people whom you know. Instead of going out for drinks, you may find yourself staying in on many Friday nights to focus on your biggest projects. You might start using Wi-Fi on airplanes to catch up on email instead of watching a movie. You may not always want to do it, but you'll find yourself doing it anyway. You'll have to control your discretionary effort, stick to it, work your tail off, and do the things you're passionate about, even when you are tired. One day, the undeniable satisfaction of getting results will outweigh the negative emotions while gritting it out.

STOP Make the YOUzone part of your daily routine. To gain momentum and avoid burnout, remember to start slowly. Look at your calendar for next week. Schedule the initial YOUzone that you created. Execute...and enjoy the benefits of being more productive.

Behavior #4: Discover Your 60Xer

I know what you might be thinking. You just learned how to accomplish a lot through the YOUzone, but you're still a little confused with how to spend your vital sixty-minute "Eat the Banana" focus session. I'm going to show you exactly what banana you should be investing your time in *right now*.

How Do You Know What Banana to Eat *Right Now*?

I'm probably the pickiest person in the world when it comes to eating produce. When I eat a banana, I prefer it to be yellow, with a little bit of green, and absolutely no brown spots. Very few bananas will meet my specific criteria. Just like there are very few bananas that are to my liking, there are very few projects that I care to spend my discretionary time doing.

The 60Xer Question

To know if it is something that you should pour your life into *right now*, ask yourself the 60Xer question *every* day:

> **In the next few months, what project has the potential of giving you sixty times return from your sixty-minute "Eat the Banana" session every day?**

I call the project that you choose a 60Xer because investing sixty minutes in it per day has compounded my results by sixty times. These are the sixty minutes that ninety percent of society are *too busy* to capitalize on. Right now, my 60Xer is investing my sixty minutes to market my speaking, facilitating, and coaching services.

 Your 60Xer

Write down your answer to the 60Xer question. In the next few months, what project has the potential of giving you sixty times return from your sixty-minute "Eat the Banana" session every day?

_____

_____

_____

_____

_____

Top Three 60Xer Responsibilities

Once you have deemed something a 60Xer, you have a lot of work ahead of you. Unfortunately, I usually underestimate the time needed to accomplish one. To help me manage time, I chart the course for my 60Xer by breaking down the top three responsibilities that I need to complete.

My 60Xer: Market my speaking, facilitating, and coaching services.

My Top Three 60Xer Responsibilities:

1. Write blog posts.
2. Build video library.
3. Create podcast.

🛑 Your Top Three 60Xer Responsibilities

Your 60Xer: _____

Your Top Three 60Xer Responsibilities:

    1. _____
    2. _____
    3. _____

Behavior #5: Schedule Your To-Dos

To be fulfilled, you will need to shine your headlights on your 60Xer responsibilities, vision, passions, and priorities. But I know what you're thinking…you also have a bunch of other never-ending projects to complete, both at home and at work—the ones you'll take care of when you're less busy.

Are We Really That Busy?

I can't count the number of times in a day when I hear people complain about how busy they are. Too often we answer, "How are you?" with, "I'm so busy." **Reality check: We are all "so busy" or feeling like we're "getting slammed."** It's no surprise that many of us fall victim to our life stressors, given the high demands that are placed on our shoulders. To fit everything in, we become completely overloaded. Being busy can be a dream killer.

Have you ever had a week when nothing seemed to go right? You left the gas station with your phone on top of your car, drove away, and smashed it. You deleted all your computer files. You spilled white Greek yogurt all over your black pants before a presentation. You locked your keys in the trunk before heading to a college basketball game. You forgot to shut the garage door and raccoons ransacked it. You left your gym locker door open and banged your head on it when you stood up. Yes, *all* of these things did happen to me, all in the span of one week, because I was too busy and lacked focus.

As I've Grown, My Calendar Has Grown

Open your calendar. Look at yesterday. Look at today. Look at tomorrow. Just like you, my calendar is full. Do you run your days, or do your days run you? Do you see yourself trending toward or away from your passions? Too often we feel like we have too many priorities and we end up saying "forget it" and do nothing. Do we actually need to learn *how to* prioritize?

> Do you run your days, or do your days run you?

When I prioritize my day, checking email or responding to random things never makes my calendar, but these tasks always seem to consume me. I tend to look at to-do lists like a squirrel. I try to do everything, but end up running in all different directions.

What interferes with your productivity? **Your calendar doesn't lie. What you schedule in your calendar is what you deem important right now.** If you're anything like me, your to-do list will always be too long. Some of your projects are seemingly huge while others are relatively small. No matter the size, it's important to stop saying that we don't have time. We're all given twenty-four hours each day.

Three Tips for Scheduling To-Dos

How we choose to schedule our time is up to us. Scheduling my to-dos has changed my life. It ensures that I end my day with fulfillment, not frustration. Here are my three tips:

1. **Use a digital calendar to create your ideal day template.** Doing this will allow you to easily repeat the day-to-day routines that you must do and should do. For example, I have the following time slots and routines blocked off every

day *(please note that this is only a template, and like every best-laid out plan, I deviate from it when necessary)*:

5:00 a.m.–7:00 a.m.	YOUzone
7:00 a.m.–8:00 a.m.	Family
8:00 a.m.–11:30 a.m.	Day Job
11:30 a.m.–1:00 p.m.	Workout and Shower
1:00 p.m.–6:00 p.m.	Day Job
6:00 p.m.–8:00 p.m.	Family
8:00 p.m.–9:30 p.m.	Check Email and Read
9:30 p.m.–5:00 a.m.	Sleep

2. **Every Sunday, add your non-routine items for the upcoming week inside your weekly template.** For example, add doctor appointments, date nights, mentorship lunches, special school events for the kids, and staff meetings.

3. **Whenever possible, schedule twenty-nine-minute meetings.** Do you block off one hour for most meetings? Think about it...Whenever you schedule a meeting or appointment in your digital calendar, the default setting is one hour. Our society has adopted one hour as the norm. Can you guess what happens when we schedule that whole hour? We manage to fill all sixty minutes with *something*, whether it's truly needed or not. After I had this aha moment, I made one major change. I shortened most of my meetings from sixty minutes to twenty-nine minutes. (Twenty-nine minutes and not thirty because I believe all meetings should end early.) Was the change successful? Yes. I've learned to be more decisive, focused, and prompt. I've freed up more time and improved results.

STOP Your Ideal Weekly Schedule

Before using a digital calendar, write your ideal weekly schedule. Write your routines, meetings, workouts, YOUzones, 60Xer, and other repetitive tasks in the "Activity" areas below. Then, write the number of minutes or hours for each activity in the "Duration" areas. When you're ready, transfer your schedule to a repetitive digital calendar and stay on track.

Activity: Duration:

Activity: Duration:

Activity: Duration:

Activity: Duration:

Activity: Duration:

Activity: Duration:

Activity: Duration:

Activity: Duration:

Behavior #6: Learn to Say No

Let's fast forward six months…You're making progress on your 60Xer, vision, passions, and priorities. You're growing. Your influence is expanding. Your network is exploding. Everyone wants your time.

Think about the last time that you were asked to make a commitment that you really weren't interested in. Did you say no right away? Did you say yes, and then later say no? Did you say yes, and then show up and later regret it? Does someone keep asking to meet with you because you keep saying maybe? Were you worried about how the other person would feel if you said no? Do you have an over-commitment problem because you say yes to everything?

My Inability to Say No

I spent some time pondering my inability to say no. Let me break down what I've learned, and how I learned it.

An acquaintance going through a career transition reached out to me to see if he could pick my brain. I quickly said yes, but unfortunately, I showed up unfocused and not present. I should've said right away, "For now, I'm currently focusing my free time on a major project. Would you like me to send you a few resources that I think could help you in the meantime?" Or, "I lead an online group coaching program called Shifting Gears Team. Would you like me to send you the details?"

Someone I'd never met asked me to meet for coffee to tell me more about a network marketing business he had started. I quickly said yes, but then I cancelled later after I looked at my overscheduled week. I should've said no right away, "Unfortunately, I've tried that business model in the past and I didn't enjoy it. Let me think about some people who might be interested."

A friend asked me to go to a sporting event during the work week. I quickly said yes, but then I cancelled late the day before so I could spend time with my family. I should've said right away, "During the week, I try to block off nights to be with my family. Let me check my calendar to see if a different game might work."

Just Say No! Don't Say Yes and Then No

You see, I'm a people pleaser. While I thoroughly enjoy connecting with people and I want to spend time with everyone, this behavior really shoots me in the foot. Unfortunately, I'm horrible at saying no and really good at halfway commitments…saying yes and then no. I'm not good at standing firm.

Saying no is *professional*—you know best what to do with your time, and saying no to others is acceptable. Saying yes and then no is *unprofessional*—whenever possible, we need to be responsible and honor our time commitments, and cancelling at the last minute is unacceptable.

If you must say no to someone and are feeling guilty about it, keep these things in mind:

- Saying no is much easier than saying yes and then no—this allows you to avoid cancelling late.
- Saying no helps you become a better leader—this allows you to invest more time into your family, into people who report directly to you, and into your customers.
- Saying no is not mean or selfish—it means you are being honest with others.
- Saying no provides laser-like focus—it allows you to concentrate on your key passions and priorities.

Stand firm. Don't be a wimp. Kill the guilt. It's ok to say no. It's ok to say, "Let me think about it." It's ok to ask for more information. It's ok to offer different options.

> Kill the guilt.
> It's ok to say no.

Oh, and by the way, it's also 100 percent ok to say yes...especially to your spouse!

Make a "Say Yes" List

It's so much easier to say no when you first know what you will most likely respond to with a yes. For me, I strive to always say yes to my values and passions.

My "Say Yes" List

- ○ I'll say yes to my family member or friend who is hurting.
- ○ I'll say yes to my kids or spouse who want quality time.
- ○ I'll say yes to my employee who is new and confused.
- ○ I'll say yes to doing some type of physical activity every day.
- ○ I'll say yes to reading something positive every morning.

STOP **Your "Say Yes" List**

Write your "Say Yes" list. Try to keep your list as lean as possible.

_____

_____

_____

_____

_____

Make a "Say No" List

If you're going to make time for you to achieve what you desire, you must know when to say no. Now that you've decided what you'll be saying yes to, it's time to create a "Say No" list. Stop attacking the wrong hill that isn't a priority, and start focusing on your values and passions. Ask yourself, "If I haven't done *it* in a month, do I need to do *it* at all?" Will you care about it next year? **Don't procrastinate about things that you can eliminate for good.**

Here is my "Say No" list:

My "Say No" List

○ I'll avoid playing basketball to minimize my injuries.
○ I'll avoid checking my phone 200+ times per day to focus on what's most important.
○ I'll avoid attending worthless meetings to spend more quality time with my colleagues.
○ I'll avoid comparing myself to others so I can avoid buying things that I don't need.
○ I'll avoid adding social media platforms that don't align with my values and passions.
○ I'll avoid worrying about everything to focus only on the things that I can control.

STOP **Your "Say No" List**

Write your "Say No" list. What will you stop doing once and for all?

_____

_____

_____

_____

_____

Stop Worrying

If you want to be successful with your "Say No" list, stop worrying about what you can't control. I'll never forget the time when Rachel accidently crashed into the left side of our garage while parking the car. She was extremely upset and shaken up about the damage to the garage. After I made sure that Rachel was ok, I said that it's pointless to worry because the damage has already been done. The garage is something that can easily be fixed.

What if you're worrying about nothing? You can't control the results of many of the things that you worry about. Think about it...if you worry for a total of one hour each day for a full year, you pretty much wasted 365 hours, or fifteen total days, worrying. What if you had invested those fifteen days into your "Say Yes" list?

> If you worry for a total of one hour each day for a full year, you pretty much wasted 365 hours, or fifteen total days, worrying.

Start Focusing

For me, reading requires only a little bit of energy, but writing takes a lot. It's easy to read every online article and e-book that comes through. While writing this book, I was receiving over 200 emails a day. As my deadline loomed, I decided to file every newsletter to read after *SHIFT* was completed. (It felt so refreshing...try it!) I finally realized that reading instead of writing was my issue and I had to get control over it. I couldn't keep adding more distractions to my calendar. If I would've kept reading and reading, I never would've finished writing. When you start to focus, you'll simplify your life.

Is It Possible to Edit Your Life?

When I was a video scout in the NBA, we would take forty-eight minutes of game footage and clip it to less than three so the players would stay focused and engaged. During the cutting process, the coaches and I would ask ourselves, "What do we really need to show the players to maximize our opportunity to win?" Every time, the coaches and I would initially pick out well over three minutes' worth of video. We had to keep trimming and trimming. Even after we'd reached our three-minute goal, all too often we'd find a clip that we liked better. At that point, we couldn't add anything without cutting something else. What do you really need to do to be fulfilled? What should you cut out of your life to achieve your vision?

More often than not, quantity kills quality...and you get run over. Moving forward, constantly edit your life through tradeoffs. Wisely exchange one thing for another. Don't add something to your life unless you can trim something out.

> Don't add something to your life unless you can trim something out.

 Write down a distraction that is holding you back from fulfillment. If you eliminated it, what action would you replace it with? Now, actually cut and replace it.

Distraction to Cut: _____

Action to Implement: _____

Behavior #7: Try New Things

During my career, I've tried a number of different jobs. Unfortunately, I was frustrated working in a factory, selling beer, coaching basketball, and selling nutrition products. As time went by, it became harder and harder to try new things. Thankfully, I kept experimenting and now I'm very satisfied with leading an athletic club, speaking, teaching, writing, and coaching. As I grew and progressed, I learned three valuable lessons…

Lesson #1: Don't Wait for a Raise or Promotion

Take a look at the job you are comfortable in now. What opportunities are within your reach in your current organization? For me, I raised my hand one day and offered to lead a key section in our new-hire orientation. After speaking at my company's national conference for a couple of years, I asked to have the role of director of training and development added to my leadership position, initially with no additional compensation.

You might be asking yourself, "Why in the world would anyone agree to accept more responsibility without additional compensation?" It brings to mind something I once heard…**Jerry Seinfeld did over 1,000 free shows before he made it big because he loved what he was doing.** Like Seinfeld, my passion for training and development was bigger than money. I'll be forever grateful that I traded some time and money to further develop what I wanted to do for the rest of my life. Today, I speak nationally.

Can you try new things in your organization? If you're stuck, be the team member always looking to help others. Know when to be flexible and take on an internal project that aligns with your passions…even if you're very busy, won't be paid, and it's not your job. Stay hungry, smile, introduce yourself to others, and always be on the lookout for projects that stretch your skills. **In your current role, always give it your all and shatter expectations.** Maybe one day you'll create the job you've always dreamed of doing inside or outside of your day job. You never know who might be watching.

Lesson #2: Be OK with People Making Fun of You

Are you holding back because you don't want your peers to make fun of you? If you're one of those people who do everything that you can to grow and advance, people will poke fun at you to your face and possibly even talk about you behind your back. I've learned to be ok with that. They make fun of you because it's easier to do than to be disciplined enough to live at a higher level. I've had my share of times when I've had colleagues approach me after a meeting and say, "Your preparation makes us look bad." If you're one of those people who try to hold others back, kindly change your thinking. Instead, see if you can be the guy or gal who comes most prepared at the next opportunity.

Lesson #3: Keep Your Heart AND Your Options Open

No matter how amazing you are, or the organization is, sometimes there aren't any opportunities. It is always important to keep your options open. If you do, you may end up on a path that takes you to places you never dreamed possible. Legendary baseball player and manager Yogi Berra said it best: **"When you come to a fork in the road, take it."**

Life flies by, and sometimes an opportunity will only present itself only once. When I heard about the opportunity to be the director of player development for the University of Utah while I was at the 2007 Final Four in Atlanta, I stayed in my hotel room for three straight nights while everyone was out celebrating. During this time, I scouted the previous year's team, wrote my cover letter, and updated my resume to ensure that I'd get the position.

I was stuck in the role I was in, so Rachel and I took this once-in-a-lifetime fork in the road that led to Utah. At the time, it was the hardest decision of our lives. We cried over leaving our families behind in Wisconsin, not knowing if or when we would return. In hindsight, it shouldn't have been such a difficult decision to make. We were newlyweds with no children or mortgage. Our families were the only thing tethering us to Wisconsin. Do you have an opportunity calling you that you should consider, seeing as it may never present itself again?

It's ok to keep juggling all the aspects that will help you figure out what you truly love. If you try something and love it, stick with it. If you try something and don't enjoy it, learn from it and make a change. If you move on from something that you didn't enjoy, look at it as an opportunity that helped promote more clarity in your life.

STOP **What task or role do you want to try that syncs with your vision, values, and passions? Write down steps that you could take to try the opportunity that you might just end up loving and doing for the rest of your life.**

_____

_____

_____

_____

_____

Behavior #8: Start Consuming Now

I'll never forget the time I was having a routine conversation with a teacher. He was upset that he had to attend a personal development in-service the next day. I asked him, "Why don't you want to go?" He replied, "It's bad timing because school is already done for the year."

Can You Wait Until Tomorrow?

From birth until you graduate from college, you'll live life for about 192,720 hours. Quickly, you realize that you don't receive a syllabus or curriculum for life. From college graduation to retirement, you have about 367,920+ hours. I don't know exactly where you are on the continuum, but I do know that it's on you to manage your own personal growth. I'm your fellow traveler to support you, but no one can do the growing for you.

When's the best time to start growing? Right now! Don't procrastinate. There may never be a perfect time to grow. **Make the decision to consume now what you'll want or need later.**

"I Don't Know How."

The great thing about learning is that everyone can do it. It doesn't matter what your background is or what you already know. If you don't understand how to consume something with respect to your vision, values, and passions, search "how-to ..." online. Take advantage of having excellent information so readily available. No more excuses.

Horizontal Growth

My daily routine for personal growth is quite rigorous, but it didn't start that way. It started in the most basic, rudimentary way possible. It started without a plan. I was given a book, and I decided to read it on the weekends when my one-year-old daughter napped. It was just me, the summer sun, and my favorite chair in the backyard. This started my love for reading. As my children grew and stopped napping, I started to reserve the bookends of my day, 5:00 a.m. and 8:00 p.m., for personal growth. I would read for hours and hours.

When I discovered the power behind cutting, pasting, sharing, applying, and filing what I was reading, I started to diversify the ways in which I'd consume self-help information. This kept learning fun and fresh. I'd listen to audiobooks in the car, watch online videos at home, read blog posts in the coffee shop, listen to podcasts on exercise machines, and read magazines while waiting for appointments.

I loved consuming anything in the self-help genre, but not with only one topic in mind. I call this approach "horizontal personal growth." I was learning as much as I could, without targeting anything specific.

Vertical Growth

My fascination for consuming self-help materials continued to grow. One year, I set goals to read twenty-four books within the year and seventy-five articles each week for fifty-two weeks. Five years later, I finally realized that it was becoming an ego thing to impress myself and others. I wasn't accomplishing anything, except for information overload. Are you on information overload?

When I contemplated about what it was that I hoped to speak, write, and coach about, I started to go somewhere again. I stopped buying a wide range of books and magazines, and stopped subscribing to so many random blogs, articles, podcasts, and videos. I decided to follow one speaker, one author, and one coach. This was the beginning of my vertical personal growth. I was learning as much as I could, specifically about speaking, writing, and coaching. The result—I listened to *my* thoughts, founded a business, wrote this book, started blogging, and booked more speaking gigs. What would you be able to accomplish if you went deep in just one, two, or three areas?

Personal Growth Budget

Is personal growth a piece of your budget? No one—not even a financial advisor—has ever asked me this question. Just like it's important to create a financial plan, it's also important to consider a personal growth budget. Over time, I've spent thousands of dollars on personal development for books, coaches, seminars, and workshops. My personal growth budget is about 5 percent of my income.

> Is personal growth a piece of your budget?

Benjamin Franklin once said, **"For the best return on your money, pour your purse into your head."** I couldn't agree with him more. It costs money to learn, but that's going to come back to you tenfold if you apply and share what you've learned. What is your personal growth budget?

STOP **Think about the area or areas of your life that you want to grow vertically in. For example, you want to become a life coach. Write down your initial personal growth budget. For example, you'll allocate 3 percent of your annual income to become a certified life coach. Commit to lifelong learning by investing in you!**

_____

_____

_____

_____

_____

Behavior #9: Mentor Up

In the summer of 2004, the Milwaukee Bucks were just coming off a tough NBA playoff loss to the Detroit Pistons. I was entering my fourth season as part of the Bucks video scouting department. As happens every off-season, staffing changes occurred. One addition to our team was Jim Boylen, a new assistant coach. We referred to him as Coach B. On his first day, I knew right away that there was something different about him. Although we only spent one season together in Milwaukee, Coach B taught me a lot. Within no time, he became my mentor because he regularly shared his experiences with me.

Nine Lessons My Mentor Taught Me about Leadership

1. **Lead yourself.** Coach B had strong personal values. He exercised, ate well, spent time with his family, and was a person of faith. You cannot lead others if you cannot lead yourself.

2. **Go first**. In my experience at the NBA and Division I level, most coaches tended to avoid the video rooms because they were dark, lacked interaction, and were not a lot of fun to be in. Coach B was different. In fact, he was the video coordinator for the Houston Rocket's two championships in the mid-'90s, long before his stint in Milwaukee. Coach B understood the importance of our department, initiated contact with me on his first day, and then continued to check in with me daily.

3. **See their potential**. Coach B saw my spark early and knew that I had the desire to do whatever it took to grow and win. He always said that he saw a lot of himself in me, which was a huge confidence boost.

4. **Know their dream**. When I was growing up, I had a dream just like every other kid. My dream was to be an NBA basketball player. Between high school and college, it finally hit me that playing professionally was not going to happen, as I could barely jump over a piece of paper. My dream quickly changed to becoming a head coach. Coach B made it a point to ask about my dream and remind me about it regularly.

5. **Share experiences with them**. In the second week, we started playing one-on-one together before the players arrived. Starting the second month, he invited Rachel and me over to his house for dinner.

6. **Evaluate their skills**. Like most coaches, Coach B gave me a number of video assignments to test my ability. However, unlike most coaches, he took me on the court to teach me the individual fundamentals the same way he taught NBA All-Stars. Immediately after, he checked for understanding by having me teach the fundamentals back to him.

7. **Provide them with feedback**. After I finished a pre- or post-game video clip, Coach B showed me what he liked, what he didn't like, and what I had missed.

8. **Keep them in-the-know**. If you look up the 2004–2005 Milwaukee Bucks team roster, my name is not on it, nor should it be because I was part-time. Even though I didn't get any public recognition, Coach B made me feel significant by constantly asking me what the team could do better and what I saw. He was the first person at this level to see me as a basketball mind.

9. **Free them**. Coach B connected me to Marquette University because he knew that for me to achieve my dream, I had to be active at practice vs. sitting in a video room. He gave me a platform to grow, without a ceiling to hold me back.

When a Leader Gives, Everyone Grows

What were the results? Coach B not only influenced my life in a positive way, but he also touched many others with his willingness to mentor and share his attitude and life experience to help them grow. When a true leader gives, everyone grows. I am convinced that he became a head coach at the University of Utah because he had inspired so many people along the way. Once I decided to stop pursuing my dream of becoming a head coach in basketball, I visualized becoming a head coach in a different industry.

Do You Need a Mentor?

Did you have your own mentor(s) as you grew and evolved into the person you are today? **A good mentor will unleash your passions, guide your growth, and encourage your success.** Mentors can play an important role in your career development. They will offer advice and share their knowledge, which is priceless. As you grow and progress, your mentoring relationships will change. How have your mentors made a positive difference in your life?

If you want to grow faster, stay open and learn from those people who have been there and done that. Today, my mentors are mostly authors, speakers, and coaches, because that's where I'm headed.

"Mentoring up" means finding people who have successfully and selflessly been where you want to go. Stop always wanting to be at the head of the class. Get uncomfortable and stretch yourself.

Where are you going? Has your mentor been there? When you find the right match, you'll quickly realize that he or she was once stuck or frustrated, too. You'll be on your way to living your potential and becoming the person you've always wanted to be.

Whose Responsibility Is It?

When I was on the alumni board at Wisconsin Lutheran College, I led the careers subcommittee. I was amazed at how many students expected their professors to reach out to different leaders and organizations for mentorship opportunities. It doesn't matter if you're a student, entrepreneur, or employee, **you must take complete responsibility to seek out passionate mentors yourself.**

What If You Can't Find a Match?

We are surrounded by mentors. Today, you have more options than any previous generation. Your mentor can be someone that you haven't met in person. Think about it…Have I met you in person? Some yes, but most of you, no. If we haven't met and you've read this far, I've been guiding your growth and encouraging your success. In essence, I have been virtually mentoring you.

Looking back at my journey, roughly 80 percent of my mentors came in the form of virtual resources. Over time, I've been fortunate enough to meet some of them in person. One day, I hope that you and I will meet face-to-face.

 Make a list of people who do what you want to do. Consider writing down one name for each of your passions and priorities. Reach out to meet with one of them today! When they commit, be on time, listen to his or

her answers, take notes, and send a handwritten thank-you note. You'll both walk away inspired to take action.

Behavior #10: Recharge Your Battery

Do you ever feel behind, exhausted, stressed, impatient, or irritable? Is your yawn another scream for coffee? Does your dessert order always start with, "I shouldn't," and always end up with you being stuffed?

Planning the FEW Fundamentals

After spending over 10,000 hours in my life enjoying tasty treats, 10,000 hours in the gym, and 10,000 hours as an athletic club leader, I've developed the following acronym and formula to help improve energy levels: FEW: Food + Exercise + Water = Energy. Stop complicating wellness and start simplifying it. Always plan the FEW fundamentals and you'll be on fire every day. Let me break it down for you...

FEW: Food + Exercise + Water = Energy

Food: What we eat for fuel affects our productivity and can make or break our entire day. I'll never forget the time I facilitated a full-day workshop at Johnson Controls International and a participant came in late, looking sluggish and lugging six full bottles of Coke, two full liters of orange juice, and a couple candy bars. That was his fuel for the day. Unfortunately, those of us who are always checking email, running to the next meeting, or feeling bogged down with a nonstop schedule, we tend to give more thought to

147

our work than to our nutrition for the day. Minimize your eating decisions. Make them before you get hungry or thirsty.

Exercise: When we think about exercise, we tend to focus on the physical benefits. For me, however, the more immediate benefit is how it improves my mood, focus, creativity, and stress levels. Former president John F. Kennedy once said, "Physical fitness is not only one of the most important keys to a healthy body, it is the basis of dynamic and creative intellectual activity." Stop allowing work to get in the way every day.

The next time you are sitting in your comfy chair and dozing off at the computer, don't check more emails…stretch and move! **Exercise is not a luxury; it's a necessity.** Find something you enjoy, make exercise a part of your job description, or schedule it with a friend every day just as you would book a meeting. Don't cancel these appointments. Watch your energy and performance levels soar.

Water: So, what can water do for productivity? Everything! In school, we learned that the body is about 65 percent water. Google lists about 500 million articles, podcasts, videos, and other resources on the benefits of water, such as more energy, younger skin, and a healthier body. Because I'll forget to, or fail to, make the time to refill, I pack multiple bottles of water every day to ensure total hydration. Find out what works for you and start being intentional about your consumption of water.

And…don't forget about sleep: I'm not an expert on sleep. However, I know from personal experience that a bad night of sleep makes me irritable, while an awesome night of sleep gives me a day filled with opportunity. Instead of telling yourself, "I'm too busy to sleep," ask yourself, "Do I want to be too busy and crabby for the rest of my life?" If you're tired all day, start taking care of yourself. Listen to your body because rest and recovery fuels growth.

You might be thinking that the FEW fundamentals seem helpful, but that you are too busy to change everything to ensure proper nutrition, exercise, water, and sleep. What is the one wellness habit that you should start right now?

The Best Way to Stay Fit and Energized When You're Busy

I'll never forget my mom's sixtieth birthday party. So many family members and friends attended, and there were many who I hadn't seen since I was in high school. Aside from "How's your family?" and "Where do you work?" I was asked another question more than any other. It essentially was, "How do you stay so fit and energized with a young family and a demanding career?"

As I was driving home later that evening, I started to think about that question. I thought about the busy people I know who also stay fit. Some of them wear fitness trackers, but not all. When I wear a fitness tracker, I over train. Some people are young, but not all. Some people receive discounts at athletic clubs through their employer or their insurance providers, but not all. Some of them even train for marathons or triathlons, but not all. I admit, when I train for competitions, I start dreading my workouts. Some people have jobs that require active movement all day, but not all. Some fit people take the stairs instead of the elevators, but not all. Some of them always eat healthy, but not all. Some play volleyball or basketball or another team sport, but not all. I kept asking myself, "How do busy/fit people stay fit? What is the common link?"

Make Fitness a Part of Your Day

Then I asked the question with respect to myself, "What do I do to stay fit and energized when I'm so busy?" After my ninety-minute drive, I finally concluded that I'm committed to one habit that has made the most positive impact on my fitness—**I make fitness a part of my day by consistently scheduling it in my calendar.** This habit continually reinforces and strengthens my consistency in maintaining fitness.

Think about it…when you want or need to do something, what is the first thing that you do? You schedule it! For me, I schedule fitness in my calendar just like I schedule a meeting with a colleague, driving my kids to school, working on a big project at work, going to a dental appointment, or taking a vacation.

I've come to the realization that all the fit and energized busy people who live in high gear do the same thing. They schedule exercise as a huge priority along with their other huge priorities. Do you think these fit, busy people always want to workout five to six days a week? Probably not. There are days when they are not feeling their best or might even be exhausted. They exercise because they receive the daily rewards of feeling happier, healthier, more productive, and more energized.

Think End of Time, Not End of Month

You can be fit and energized, too. All the excuses that we use to avoid wellness are typically the actual reasons why we should focus on being well. Take the time to be well. The people close to you want you around for a very long time. If you don't take the time to make yourself a priority and are always feeling tired, you will likely end up less productive and more exhausted. If you schedule your workouts and follow the FEW fundamentals, you'll have more energy, and that will directly translate into more quality time.

If you're worried that taking this time for yourself seems selfish, think about this…Would you rather be around energizing or draining people? I'm guessing you picked energizing. Those same people want to be around energizing people, too. Manage your energy, not your time! The number one thing that you can give your family, friends, and colleagues is your energy. Start now. Live well short-term so that you can lead well long-term. Build a life in which you can get work done and stay healthy at the same time.

> Build a life in which you can get work done and stay healthy at the same time.

Recharge your battery by making wellness a part of your plan for personal growth. Download the Planning the FEW Worksheet at:
DerekDeprey.com/manage-your-energy-not-your-time

Move. Grow. Achieve.

I hope that my sharing the top ten behaviors that moved me from being frustrated to being fulfilled has helped you to think about your own personal growth plan. None of us wakes up one day knowing what we want to do for the rest of our lives. For me, it all started with that interview question, "What is your plan for personal growth?" That was such a powerful question; I truly think now that it might be the most powerful interview question that exists. I make it a point to ask that of everyone I interview, and I usually get a blank stare for an answer. I believe that most candidates have never thought about their own personal growth, or perhaps they don't fully understand what personal growth is all about. Most don't have a plan on how to develop themselves. I'm here to offer you a personal growth plan that should help to move you to fulfillment…for the rest of your life. Move. Grow. Achieve.

Your Personal Growth Behaviors

Think back to your vision…once again, in the blank diagram, write where you are now in the "From Frustrated" circle. Then write where you want to be in the "To Fulfilled" circle. Next, with respect to the ten *Move to Grow* behaviors that are listed below, circle the top three behaviors that you should do or focus on. *If you have a behavior that you want to focus on that is not in my top ten, feel free to add it.* When you're ready, transfer the corresponding numbers of your circled behaviors into your "Behaviors" arrow.

1. Do It Afraid
2. Set a Deadline
3. Commit to Daily YOUzones
4. Discover and Do Your 60Xer
5. Schedule Your To-Dos
6. Say No
7. Try New Things
8. Start Consuming Now
9. Mentor Up
10. Recharge Your Battery

Move to Grow in Action – Derek

BEHAVIORS

FROM FRUSTRATED:
I'm saying yes to too many things outside my personal vision, passions, and priorities.

4, 6, 9

TO FULFILLED:
I will help to move one million people from frustrated to fulfilled through books, keynotes, workshops, and coaching.

Move to Grow in Action – _____

BEHAVIORS

FROM FRUSTRATED:

TO FULFILLED:

Finally, execute your top three behaviors to continue your momentum of going from where you are to where you want to be. Realize that as you grow and transform, your focus areas will change. Every quarter, it's important to work hard, assess, and tweak accordingly, but don't be obsessed. Promise me that you'll continue to have fun along the way.

Can You Be Your Best without Being Obsessed?

Have you ever been obsessed with something? I surely have been. In sixth grade, I was obsessed about eating one Whatchamacallit candy bar every single day. In seventh grade, I was obsessed with collecting as many Michael Jordan and Magic Johnson sports cards as financially possible. In eighth grade, I was obsessed with winning Sega Genesis basketball video games. By far, my biggest obsession growing up, however, was to become the best basketball player that I could be.

"How Do You Try to Be Your Best without Allowing the Pursuit of Excellence to Become Your IDOL?"

Coach Jack Bennett—an incredible mentor, head basketball coach of the UW-Stevens Point back-to-back national championship teams, national coach of the year, and an even better person than professional—provoked some deep thought for me when he asked me a powerful question. He said, "How do you try to be your best without allowing the pursuit of excellence to become your IDOL?" When I received his email, I dropped everything that I was doing to read it again.

Was My Book Becoming My IDOL?

After a day had passed, I was a little concerned that I was allowing the pursuit of *SHIFT* to become my idol. Two days later, I did a 180-degree turnaround and began to think that writing my book was simply a hobby. After three days, I told myself that I was dedicated, but not exactly obsessed. Four days later, I was terribly confused.

Was I Dedicated or Obsessed?

To clarify some things in my mind, I did some research on the words *dedicated* and *obsessed*. Being dedicated is staying devoted to a task or purpose—dedication is viewed as positive. Being obsessed is filling the mind continually, intrusively, and to a troubling extent—obsession is viewed as negative.

But is obsession really negative? From my experiences, there are good and bad elements of obsession. It can be bad when you have a painful addiction, are never satisfied, try to be the best at everything, rarely recover, or neglect other important things in your life. Obsession can be good when you focus on your passions, try to be the best version of yourself, strive to reach your potential, enjoy every minute of your routine, celebrate your wins, or make regular progress.

Today, I wouldn't be compensated for my passion if I didn't have the drive, determination, resilience, and perseverance to become a better leader, speaker, and writer. So the question still remains... am I obsessed or just really dedicated?

The Light Bulb Moment

The light bulb went on for me when I reread Coach Bennett's question again. His question actually asks *how* you can try to be your best, not *whether you can* try to be your best..."without allowing the pursuit of excellence to become your IDOL." He implied that you absolutely *can* be your best without allowing the pursuit of excellence to become your idol. It is not an all-or-nothing proposition. Realizing this, I felt like I had removed a ton of bricks from my back. Pursuing excellence in a healthy and productive way *is* possible! There are constructive and beneficial ways to pursue your dreams.

It takes a tremendous amount of dedication to be your best. I wouldn't have finished *SHIFT* without being a little bit obsessed, as well as being dedicated to the process. Truth be told, waking up at 5:00 a.m. every single morning could probably be described as an obsession. Over the last couple of years, however, I've tried to make my obsession work for me, not against me.

So, can you be your best without being a little obsessed? Not really. But can you try to be your best without allowing the pursuit of excellence to become your idol? Most definitely.

Who Does Your Obsession Benefit?

Let's go back to my early basketball obsession. My obsession with practicing three to four hours per day inspired a number of my other teammates to do the same. Today, I'm hoping that my obsession over the ten behaviors will inspire others to seek personal growth at the highest possible level.

According to football legend Vince Lombardi, **"Individual commitment to a group effort—that is what makes a team work, a company work, a society work, a civilization work."** In high school, our most dedicated players helped each other become the best team possible. During Coach Bennett's national championships, his dedication to pouring himself into his players and coaches, both on and off the court, fueled their winning runs.

If you move yourself to pursue excellence, you'll move others to do the same. Does your obsession benefit only you, or can you help others along the way?

Focus on Today

Growth is neither easy nor an accident, but it's worth it. It's the result of just the right attitude, passion, and execution. Most people notice wins, attitude, and passion, but few of them notice practice, effort, or execution. You've learned that execution is your gas pedal for growth. Now, it is essential for you to capitalize and apply. You're excited…so go do it! Don't wait until after the weekend. Executing your solid plan now is better than waiting for a perfect plan later. Make today the day.

> Executing your solid plan now is better than waiting for a perfect plan later.

Become the Person with Whom You Want to Spend the Rest of Your Life

The APE formula is complete. You've learned how to adopt a positive mindset, personalize your ambitions, and exercise meaningful action. In the next chapter, you'll *SHIFT* into the fifth and final gear to become the individual that you want to spend the rest of your life being. You'll create a lasting ID that you actually admire and respect. Life is not a dress rehearsal. You can fulfill your ideal life *while* executing your passions. You'll stop separating your passions and priorities from life demands. Instead, you'll learn how to apply work–life fusion vs. work–life balance. With integrated living, you'll be happier, healthier, and wealthier.

Press on and prosper.

"Execution" Key Moves

- Personalize your plan for personal growth with some or all the following behaviors:

    - 1. Do It Afraid
    - 2. Set a Deadline
    - 3. Commit to Daily YOUzones
    - 4. Discover and Do Your 60-Xer
    - 5. Schedule Your To-Dos
    - 6. Say No
    - 7. Try New Things
    - 8. Start Consuming Now
    - 9. Mentor Up
    - 10. Recharge Your Battery

- Start today

Remember...work through this book at your own pace. Don't just add *SHIFT* to your bookshelf. Take notes as you go. If you would prefer to write in a workbook, please visit: **DerekDeprey.com/ShiftBookResource**s for the complimentary download.

STOP Write down the *first thing* from this chapter's content that you will move to act on.

_____

_____

_____

_____

_____

SHIFT Roadmap: From Execution to Fusion

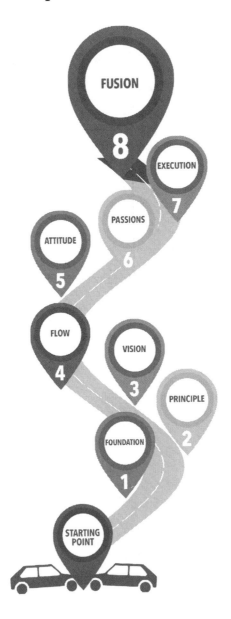

CHAPTER EIGHT

FUSION:
FULFILL YOUR IDEAL LIFE

*"The master in the art of living makes little distinction
between his work and his play, his labor and his
leisure, his mind and his body, his information and his
recreation, his love and his religion. He hardly knows
which is which. He simply pursues his vision of excellence
at whatever he does, leaving others to decide whether he is
working or playing. To him, he is always doing both."*

– James A. Michener

On a Friday afternoon, I stopped for my daily YOUzone at a Milwaukee coffee destination, Colectivo. Anticipating an afternoon filled with efficiency, I ordered a medium roast coffee—straight black, with no room for cream—settled in to a place free from distraction, fired up my laptop, and set out some leadership and personal development articles that I intended to read. As I began reading, I noticed that a gentleman in his mid-sixties at the next table was constantly looking over at me.

"Are You One of Those People Who Just Works All the Time?"

After about fifteen minutes passed, I began to wonder why he was studying me. I received my answer when he asked, without introducing himself and with a mouth full of scone, "Are you one of those people who just works all the time?"

My immediate reaction was sheer surprise. I pondered the question for a moment after realizing that it was a really valid question. I shook my head to disagree and proceeded to tell him about my family and career. After the gentleman left, I paused in my work and reflected on the question again..."Are you one of those people who just works all the time?"

For the next hour, I reflected on my work–life balance. I had an uneasy feeling about it, until I pulled out a pen and paper. I spent some time defining the following words that we use in our everyday language: work, life, and balance. That afternoon, I left with the realization that my life was not about work–life balance; rather, it was about *life* itself.

Let me show you how work and life don't have to compete, starting with *work*.

"It Must Be Nice to Start *Work* So Late."

It's a routine day. My alarm goes off at 5:00 a.m. I wake up and head to the coffee shop to knock out my biggest project of the day. Two hours later, I head back home to help my daughters get ready for school while I get ready for work. At 8:00 a.m. sharp, my daughters run to the corner and pretend that a bus will be picking them up...but it's only me. We drive to school, and each of us chooses our favorite Kidz Bop song to hear. Exactly three songs later, we arrive at school for drop-off. Finally, three blocks later, at 8:20 a.m., I walk into work to start my day job.

Over the years, I've jotted down the following phrases that people have said to me as I walked in or out of work:

- "It must be nice to start work so late."
- "Banker's hours, huh? You're just rollin' in now?" (while staring at his or her watch...)
- "Are you sleepin' in again? You're rarely in your office. I usually see you walking around."
- "Are you working out again?"
- "You're leaving already?"
- "You've been out a lot this week. Do you ever work?"

Just Stop

I bet you can relate. Unfortunately, I've been guilty of saying the same types of things to people once in a while. In fact, I've experienced this at every job I've ever had. So, why do we do this? Do we think it's a way to develop a relationship? If so, bad move. Why bring someone down by implying that they are doing something wrong? If this is you, just stop. All it does is irritate people when you create guilt for them for not working enough. What I've noticed is that the people who make the negative statements are usually the same ones asking how to be more successful.

What Does *Work* Even Mean?

When someone asks me, "Do you ever work?" I often think to myself, "What does work even mean to you?" To me, work is a fulfilling activity involving mental or physical effort to achieve a desired result. Just like you get to *choose* your definition of success, values, vision, attitude, passions, and execution, you get to *choose* what work means to you.

🛑 Your Definition of Work

What is your definition of work? Reflect and write it down.

_____

_____

_____

_____

_____

Perception is *Not* Always Reality

Now that you've determined your own definition of work, you may have come to the realization that some people are night owls and prefer to come in to work later in the morning. Some people are morning people and prefer to come in early. Some people are all-day people, and they come and go to recharge and recover. **Don't judge a path until you've walked it.**

Fortunately, most people are uplifting and say, "Good morning! How are you?" If someone has something negative to say to greet you, don't get defensive. Instead, take a deep breath, smile, and remember why you do what you do.

What goes through my mind when I hear these things? While I don't usually respond out loud, I confidently think them through and remind myself that I'm doing the right work for me. Here are a few examples.

- "It must be nice to start work so late."
  - Me: "It is! I try to respond to emails before I walk in the door so that I can be present during the day."

- "Banker's hours, huh?"
  - Me: "Yep! I'm extremely blessed to be able to drive my kids to school every day."

- "You're just rollin' in now?" (while staring at his or her watch…)
  - Me: "I am! This morning, one of my girls had a Valentine's Day party at school, and it was a blast."

- "Are you sleepin' in again?"
  - Me: "Yes. I'm very consistent with going to bed and waking up to ensure seven hours of sleep a night."

- "You're rarely in your office. I usually see you walking around."
  - Me: "Correct. I'm lucky to have a mix of sitting and moving in my leadership role."

- "Are you working out again?"
  - Me: "You bet. I schedule my daily workouts just like any other daily meetings. The workouts energize me and make me more productive."

- "You've been out a lot this week. Do you ever work?"
  - Me: "You're right! For privacy, I planned my managers' performance reviews off-site for a couple hours each day this week."

- "You're leaving already?"
  - Me: "Absolutely! I'm going to visit Santa and go on a sleigh ride through the city with my family. My children have been asking about it eagerly for days."

My advice to you: be confident and feel secure. You're doing amazing things out there…*on a schedule that works for you.*

"I Need Better Work–Life Balance."

Now that we know it's best not to judge the schedule of others, let's spend some time on another component of accomplishing what you strive for most. I often hear people say, "I need better work–life balance," or, "I don't know how to juggle my job and my family."

Are you one of these people? I am. If you are, too, don't feel bad. According to Google, there are over 108 million search results with varying definitions and philosophies for work–life balance. Just to make sure that we are on the same page, let's review the definitions for work and then add the definitions for life and balance.

To me, work is a fulfilling activity involving mental or physical effort to achieve a desired result. Life is the condition that distinguishes people, animals, and plants from inorganic matter, including through the capacity for growth and change. Balance is an even distribution of weight.

Is Balance Even Possible?

Before you can answer that question fairly, try asking yourself, "Where do you need to pay more attention?" Do you need to spend more time on self-reflection, date nights with your spouse, exercise, developing the skills that you need for your next promotion, or something else?

STOP **Where do you need to pay more attention? Reflect and write down your answer(s).**

_____

_____

_____

_____

_____

Are you paying as much attention as you want to the area(s) that you just wrote down? Most likely, you're not, because you're striving to create a balance in too many areas. If you often struggle to focus your time on those areas, you might be saying yes to things that you don't really care about, and saying no to the things that genuinely matter to you. When I try to balance and juggle too many things, I start to get frustrated, distracted, and overwhelmed, and I eventually burn out. Have you been in this situation yourself?

Balance Creates Competition

Remember, balance is an even distribution of weight. Why is this simple definition so important when it pertains to one's work and life? **You can't achieve an exact balance, or an even distribution, between your life at home and your time at work. It creates competition and confusion.** Let's go back to the foundation and find some clarity.

 ## Personal Values vs. Work Values

Grab your list of your personal core values that you formed in chapter one. Rewrite your personal values below. Next, think about the things that you value at work. When you're ready, write down your work values.

Your Personal Values

-
-
-
-
-

-
-
-
-
-

Your Work Values

-
-
-
-
-

-
-
-
-
-

Now spend the next few moments comparing and contrasting your personal values with your work values. Do you split time equally between work and life? Do your work values compete with or complement your personal values? If your work values compete, you're probably wishing for another day between Saturday and Sunday, and it might be time to look for a new career or tweak your current one. If some of your work values complement your personal values, you're on the right track to being fulfilled. The ideal situation is to match 100 percent of your personal values with your work values.

What Is Work–Life Fusion?

Work–life balance means that your work and personal values are frequently in competition. Work–life fusion means that your work and personal values are in sync.

> Work–life balance means that your work and personal values are frequently in competition. Work–life fusion means that your work and personal values are in sync.

To help understand this better, take a moment and visualize a puzzle with only two pieces. One piece is labeled "Work Values" and the other "Personal Values." If your personal values are completely different than your work values, your puzzle pieces won't link together.

If your personal values are relatively similar to your work values, you can complete your puzzle by connecting or fusing the two pieces.

Fusion is the process of joining two or more things together to form one entity.

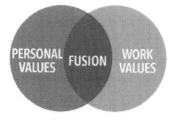

Work–life balance is about feeling stressed by trying to do a little bit of everything. This leads to trying to be all things to all people. Work–life fusion is about living your ideal life by focusing on what truly matters to *you*. Let go of the rigid boundaries that currently exist between your work and your personal life.

> Work–life balance is about feeling stressed by trying to do a little bit of everything. This leads to trying to be all things to all people. Work–life fusion is about living your ideal life by focusing on what truly matters to *you*.

Why Is Work–Life Fusion Important?

It's important to match your personal core values with your work values so you can invest the majority of your time on what's important to you. **The more time that you spend on what's important to you, the more likely you'll be fulfilled and living work–life fusion.**

According to a study published in the journal *Human Relations*, researchers from Ball State University and Saint Louis University found, "In the long run, it may be better to allow employees' minds to wander and take occasional phone calls from home rather than set up policies that establish strict and inflexible boundaries, which could discourage the development of functional ways to juggle both."

> If your values in life are similar to your values at work, the boundaries should be blurry.

If your values in life are similar to your values at work, the boundaries should be blurry. Blending together what needs to get done day to day both at work and at home will let you live the life you've been striving for from the beginning.

STOP **What could you do to better sync your personal values with your work values? For example, you might schedule a values-based conversation with your manager or spouse.**

_____

_____

_____

_____

_____

"I Have the Day Off Today, but I Have to Work Most of the Day."

If you're still a bit skeptical about work–life fusion and now wondering when you'll ever *stop* working, just stay with me. If you're currently thinking, "There is no way I'll ever blend work and life because I'd be a workaholic," let me clarify. **Fusion is *not* about being a workaholic.** A workaholic is someone who works 24/7 while ignoring family, friends, and other obligations. **Fusion is about laser-focusing on your values and passions.**

I'll never forget the time when I was on a flight to Florida to speak at a leadership event. As soon as the plane landed, I sent a text to Shane Crawford, my friend and the person who hired me, so that he would know I had arrived and was available to help with setup.

"Thank you!" he replied. "I'm at the tram to pick you up and will give you a tour of the area right away." "Perfect," I said. He went on to say, "I am off today, but I have to work most of the day...so let's check the room that you'll be speaking in." I read his reply again to make sure I hadn't misread it or misunderstood it. Nope, he meant it. He had to work all day on his day off.

This Is NOT Work–Life Fusion

Have you ever spent most of your day off working? Do you have a hard time turning off when you get home? If so, this is NOT an example of work–life fusion. If you're off, be off.

One week after my trip, I led a quarterly offsite meeting with all my managers, team leaders, and sales reps. During that meeting, it dawned on me—and really amazed me—that four of the twelve people were supposed to be off that day. They still attended with energy and enthusiasm because they're passionate about what we do.

Again, this is also NOT an example of work–life fusion. If you manage a staff and some of them are on vacation, allow them to enjoy their time away.

Do you struggle to leave work behind while you are supposed to be living life? I must admit, I do, too. Unfortunately, I used to think that working while on vacation was a cool thing to do. For example, earlier in my career, I'd go into the office on my off days, creating the illusion that I worked harder and worked more than anyone else. Starting today and together with you, let's hold each other accountable to setting a better example for our future leaders.

Wait...Is Working Ever Ok While You're Off?

You might be wondering if working at home is ever ok when you're done for the day or on vacation. Unfortunately, there isn't an easy answer. I strongly believe that the answer greatly depends on the person and his or her situation. There may be a time when working after you're done for the day will help you so that you can take a morning off to volunteer, visit a friend to hangout, or do something else. Or, it might give you back some family time so you're not working late every night when the vacation is over and you're back at work.

If you enjoy your work and are drawn to spending a lot of your free time doing it, taking work home is ok, but don't multitask when your loved ones want to be with you. Work–life fusion is not being on your phone at home incessantly checking your email when your kids want to play, or firing up your laptop as soon as you walk in the door. Strive to take out your work when your family is away or after they are sleeping so that you can be 100 percent present when they are awake. Be in the moment with what you choose to do.

"I Wish I Could Go Back and Really Capture the Moment."

One morning, I had coffee with my friend, Art Flater, to catch up on all things work and life. Not long into our conversation, he shared a story about coaching his son's basketball team. He had come to realize that their last game was actually the last time that he would ever coach his son. Unfortunately, he didn't truly realize it until a day or two after the game. "I wish I could go back and really capture the moment," he said.

This really got me thinking. How many things have passed by where I wish I could go back and truly capture the moment? I came to realize that there had been many moments that I have lived for the last time. There was the last time when I worked for the Brewers, Bucks, University of Utah, and Marquette University. There was the last time I lived in my hometown of Manitowoc, Wisconsin. There are, in fact, many things that I have done for the last time. Like my friend Art, I don't remember capturing the special moments before I left, because like most people, I was already on to the forthcoming moments in my mind.

The rest of that week, I continued asking myself the question, "How many things have passed me by where I wish I could go back and truly capture the moment?"

When Ellie was in second grade, she no longer reached for my hand when we crossed the street for school drop-off. When did she stop doing that? Thankfully, Mia still reaches for my hand. How long will that sweet innocent gesture continue? Neither of them will initiate giving me a kiss anymore before they run off to play with their friends at the playground. When did the kisses stop? I honestly don't remember, but I know that I miss those simple moments. As a third grader, Ellie attended zoo classes by herself, while Mia, a kindergartener, still preferred going with a grownup. I don't remember capturing my final time in zoo class with Ellie. Will I remember to capture the last moment with Mia? In third grade, it is rare when parent volunteers are needed at school. I'm sad to say that I don't remember really living in the last moment of volunteering in Ellie's class. In kindergarten, parents are requested fairly often…and I am determined to live those moments with Mia, knowing that someday they will come to an end. I so want to capture the moment before she grows up enough that she has no need for a parent helper in her class. Mia is likely our last child.

It's time to realize that all the little things, while they're growing up, are actually going to be the big things, looking back. **Now is the time to start waking up to live the moments!**

If You're Not Present First, You Can't Capture the Last Moment

Unfortunately, we don't always know it will be the last time for something until it's too late. However, if you're cognizant of this fact and you pay attention, there is greater likelihood that you can enjoy firsts and lasts. I am going to pay proper attention to the things that have had their first times, so that I can capture the moment of their last time. Recall that fusion is not about working when your children or friends want to play.

Remembering back, there was a first family snuggle. There was a first time roller skating as a family. There was a first time creating art projects at a museum with my girls. There was a first time when Ellie performed in a theater show. There was a first time when Mia participated in a gymnastics showcase. There was even a first family selfie. For all those things, there will also be a last time. I might be able to catch the last time only when I pay close attention and remain present in the moment.

STOP The Moments You *Won't* Miss

Write down some first and last moments that happened in your lifetime.

_____

_____

_____

_____

_____

Write down some *foreseeable* first and last moments. **Hold on to this list for reference and make a point to be there to capture the moments.**

_____

_____

_____

_____

_____

My Daily Notification

Having just written down some of the moments that you don't want to miss, if you're anything like me, you might still forget about some. People often say that time flies, and I always nod my head and say, "It sure does." Can you relate?

On a random day in 2013, I was scrolling down my Facebook feed and noticed that some friends were sharing random photo memories—children's birthdays, parents' anniversaries, and work milestones. I smiled and really enjoyed the posts. Immediately, I wondered what triggered them to post the memories. Soon after, I noticed that there was a Timehop logo in the corner of each of the pictures. Timehop is an app that collects old photos and posts from social media and distributes the past.

I Had to See It to Believe It

While I'm not a big fan of receiving notifications and interruptions on my phone, I couldn't help but download the app. Every day, I receive a notification with some memorable pictures...*On this day, one year ago, you were at the zoo; two years ago, you and Rachel celebrated your wedding anniversary; three years ago, Ellie graduated from kindergarten; and four years ago, Mia saw her first rainbow.* The moments are real. The moments go fast.

Timehop helped to change my perspective and forced me to look at what I was missing. I needed to stop staying at my day job until 7:00 p.m. a couple of nights per week. At first, I felt uncomfortable leaving earlier. Despite my anxiety, this daily notification kept me in the moment and helped me get home earlier.

"Don't Ever Miss That Again, Daddy."

Timehop definitely helps with fusion, keeping my values at the top of my mind, and staying present, but it doesn't remind me about everything.

One day after I came home from work, Mia blurted out, "Don't ever miss that again, Daddy." Confused, I said, "Don't ever miss what?" Mia said, "Today was bring your child to work day...and you didn't bring me." I'll never forget to put that day in my calendar again. The lesson: don't hesitate to involve your kids in your work. They are proud of you and want to be a part of as many aspects of your life as you can muster. For example, let them help you with your presentation, let them decorate your office, or let them deliver the mail to coworkers.

While I didn't like to hear, "Don't ever miss that again, Daddy," from my four-year-old, I do look forward to hearing, "Daddy, that was the best day ever," over and over and over again.

"Daddy, That Was the Best Day Ever."

One summer, I blocked off thirty minutes of time to go watch my daughter's swimming lesson at the gym. During lesson time, the pool is always packed with parents and their young swimmers. A few minutes into the lesson, Jeff Kempen, the maintenance technician, walked through the pool area and stopped by my chair to say hello. Moments later, I heard him say, "Derek, look up!"

I immediately looked up and said, "What?" He shook his head and said, "Look at all of the parents. They're all on their phones, and not one of them is watching their child swim." I was stunned and said, "Wow, you're right...and thank you for pointing that out! I'm totally guilty of this!"

Ever since that moment, I had wanted to block off an entire day to allow my kids to create our itinerary for the day. So, one year, during our annual staycation, I did just that. I blocked out a full twenty-four hours to be with Rachel and the girls. We didn't do any work at all; instead, we only participated in kid-directed fun.

I started out by asking Ellie and Mia what they wanted to do on our special day. They gave me quite the list, and we ended up doing pretty much everything. We played Legos, dressed American Girl dolls, went to the city pool, kicked the soccer ball around outside, created an obstacle course at the gym, made art projects, and ate at their favorite pizza place. They wanted to end the day with a sleepover, so they could fall asleep watching the movie *Barbie and the Dream House*. As requested, we hauled out all the stuffed animals, sleeping bags, pillows, and snacks, and headed downstairs to our special sleepover sanctuary in the basement.

After we got comfortable, Ellie quietly said something so small, but ever so meaningful. She said, "Daddy, that was the best day ever." At that moment, I couldn't focus on the movie, or on the articles I was about to read, or even the yummy snacks. I was overwhelmed by how consequential both being present and being in the moment really is to others.

According to a study by the *Journal of Marriage and Family*, **the sheer amount of time that parents spend with their kids, ages three to eleven, has virtually no relationship to how children turn out and a minimal effect on teens. The quality of time spent with kids, however, did make an important impact.** I thought about what being present had meant to my impressionable young daughters. I spent the hour before we drifted to sleep thinking about the benefits that I received on this extraordinary day—increased focus, productivity, and happiness. Ellie was right! I, too, had the best day ever, just being 100 percent present.

How Do You Become More Present?

I have to admit that unlike just about every article that I've read about being present, I didn't use any special mindfulness or breathing exercises to be more present with my family that entire day. Instead, I just blocked off the time and committed to doing it. Quite simply, I decided to focus my full attention on exactly where I wanted it to be that day.

Again, ask yourself: "Where do I need to pay more attention?"

Is it possible to cherish it all in the whirlwind that we live in? It may be unrealistic to think that we can capture everything, but we all can absolutely increase our awareness. I'll be forever thankful for my friend who woke me up by saying, "I wish that I could go back and capture the moment." For the rest of our lives, there will be many firsts and lasts. I'll make the time for these magical moments because I don't know for sure when it may be the last time.

Blending It All Together

Take a deep inhale. Now let it out. Work–life fusion is a lot closer to you than you think. Now that you have a basic understanding of work–life fusion, you're probably wondering how to live it. If you've read the book in its entirety to this point, you've already learned how. You live work–life fusion by blending your crash, values, principle, and vision.

For example, my crash and cues helped me solidify my foundational personal values—attitude, passions, and execution. Choosing to commit to the *Move to Grow* principle led me to visualize my preferred future, adopt a positive mindset, discover and personalize my ambitions, and execute the daily behaviors that align with my values.

My ID

Like the roads we travel on, my values interconnect. See the Venn diagram, which represents unity. The big circles are my values. The intersection of my values is the middle of the diagram, which characterizes my ID.

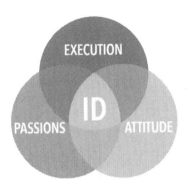

All your values, passions, and actions are fluid and consistent both inside and outside of work. You don't turn them on and off. For example, I strive to grow by reading, writing, thinking, applying, and sharing at home and at work. I strive toward wellness by being cognizant of my nutrition and exercise choices at home and at work. I strive to be in touch with, and pay attention to, my family, friends, and coworkers at home and at work. See the ID diagram inside the fusion diagram.

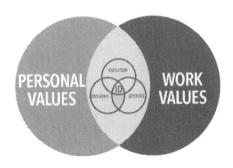

🛑 Your ID

Now it's your turn to create your ID. Take out your personal values. If you have three personal values, write one personal value in each circle below. If you have more than three personal values, simply draw your own diagram in the blank area with the number of circles you need. Write one personal value in each circle.

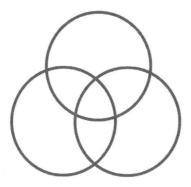

If you're regularly living in the moment with respect to your values, you're most likely well on your way toward living your definition of success. Your completed diagram represents the life that you've always wanted.

How Do You Evaluate Work–Life Fusion?

Outside of just intuitively knowing whether you are living your values and passions, I've developed the following two ways for you to evaluate your work–life fusion: the Question of Passion and the Move Matrix.

Question of Passion

People sometimes ask me, "What is your own statement of purpose or personal mission statement?" Typically, I respond with, "I have something close to that. It's called my Question of Passion."

My Question of Passion is, "Am I executing my passions with a positive attitude?" In my Question of Passion, all three of my personal values are represented. A Question of Passion should tie in your personal values and passions in one way or another.

A statement is a statement, that's all. In question form, you're evaluating yourself. The question forces you to respond to yourself with a yes, no, on track, or off track. If you can confidently answer yes or on track, then you're most likely living work–life fusion. To keep my question at the top of my mind, I typed it as my computer desktop backgrounds at home and at work.

STOP What's Your Question of Passion?

Reflect and then write down your Question of Passion. Keep it with you at all times.

_____

_____

_____

_____

_____

Move Matrix

Now that you've learned the basic evaluation, I'm going to show you a more detailed assessment called the Move Matrix. Before we go further, let me describe the matrix. The vertical axis has your Passions and the horizontal axis is the level of your Execution for each passion or priority. The top of the matrix on the vertical axis is high while the bottom is low. The horizontal left axis is low while the right is high. See the Move Matrix diagram.

MOVE MATRIX

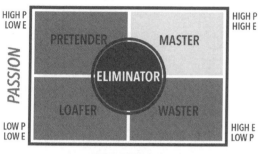

EXECUTION

These are the following items within the Move Matrix:

A **loafer** is a couch potato, or a person who hasn't found what he or she loves and doesn't work hard at much of anything. This person has low passion and low execution. Envision the loafer box with a person being lazy.

A **waster** is a busy person who spends time on unnecessary things he or she doesn't necessarily enjoy, all while accomplishing nothing. This person has low passion and high execution. Envision the waster box full of dots or menial tasks.

A **pretender** is a hypocrite or person who doesn't do what he or she says. This person has high passion and low execution. Envision the pretender box with Say ≠ Do.

A **master** is a captain or person who is in control of his or her life. This person has high passion and high execution. Envision the master box with three dots or things that matter to you.

Unfortunately, people tend to think they are masters in areas that they are really pretenders. For example, if spending time with my family is a high passion to me, yet I don't really spend any time with them, I would fall into the pretender category. I'm exercising low execution on a high passion or priority.

The **eliminator** circle represents a trash can. If something falls in the gray areas, you have a choice—move it to the master box or move it to the eliminator trash can. Move it or lose it! Avoid the gray areas.

Your goal is to have 100 percent of your passions and priorities in the master box. See diagram with my ID inside the master box.

My Move Matrix

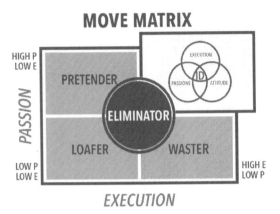

MOVE MATRIX

HIGH P
LOW E

PRETENDER

PASSION

ELIMINATOR

LOAFER   WASTER

LOW P
LOW E

HIGH E
LOW P

EXECUTION

🛑 **Your Move Matrix**

Complete the blank Move Matrix diagram. Reflect and write your answers to the following questions in the boxes:

- With respect to your life, what do you currently do in each box? Write a short list in each box.
- How do you currently feel in the Loafer, Pretender, and Waster boxes? Write one emotion in each of the three boxes. If you don't like what you feel, be mindful about these negative emotions so that you can make decisions that bring about positive emotions.
- How do you *want* to feel in the Master box? Write the top emotion that you want to feel in the Master box.
- What do you have to do in the Master box to feel your top emotion from the previous question? Is the answer to this question anchored in living your values, passions, and

priorities that you wrote down in your ID? If so, draw your ID in the Master box.

MOVE MATRIX

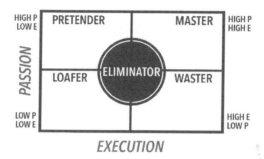

"Your Family is Really Lucky."

Now that you've learned what work–life fusion is and why it's important, and you've been able to assess where you are, you might be thinking, "Derek, you just fell into a great setup to make this fusion thing work."

I'll never forget the time when I was giving my friend, Coach Jim Gordon, a tour of the athletic club. It just so happened to be at the same time when Rachel was with our children in the pool area. Coach Gordon said, "Your family is really lucky. You get to raise your children at the club. What a great way to live your life."

After I thought about his words for awhile I realized that we do have a unique situation and we're truly blessed. This, however, was not always the case. As you've read, I wasn't always living my ideal life. I made a decision to *SHIFT* and move what was standing in my way. It took a lot of hard work and sacrifice, but I wouldn't trade it for anything. If you don't like what is standing between you and your ideal life, move it.

> If you don't like what is standing between you and your ideal life, move it.

It Takes a Team to Live the Dream

Even after I moved the jobs that were in my way, my personal and work values didn't truly sync until I realized that it takes a team to live the dream. A lot of people ask me, "How do you accomplish so much?" After some deep thought, I've come to the realization that it starts with my rock-solid team at home. Who is on your team?

Day in and day out, I could never do what I do without Rachel, the best team player I could ever ask for. She's taught me that I don't have to run away from my life to execute my passions...and that we can do it together. Because of Rachel, I intentionally do what I love in my day-to-day living. I don't cram these things in. Unfortunately, I made some major mistakes before I finally figured this out.

My Dumbest Question of All Time

On June 28, 2008, our eldest daughter Ellie was born, and our lives changed forever. Our family was overwhelmed with excitement and happiness. Our brand-new baby daughter changed our lives in a way we had never imagined; we had become a family of three. Life was good, and we were living the dream. Then, one month later, I asked my wife an innocent question. One that I will never forget..."Rachel, what do you do all day?"

Talk about rookie mistakes that new dads make. I had already hit the motherload. While I don't remember the exact response that I received, outside of, "Really, Derek?" I vividly recall the look she gave me that I totally deserved, and never want to see again.

My Most Stupid Statement of All Time

Fast forward three years...you would think that I would've learned my lesson. It was a beautiful fall day in October of 2011, a couple of months after our youngest daughter Mia was born. Our oldest daughter was now three, so I considered myself quite the parenting veteran. Not so much—having two children in diapers created a whole new chaos that we hadn't known.

One day, I came home from work and said, "I think because I bring in the money, your job is to do all the stuff at home." Again, Rachel was incredibly calm, but I couldn't have been more mistaken. I couldn't bring home anything unless Rachel always gave to us her heart and soul, along with her homemaking skills and her best-ever mommy skills.

Looking back, I'm a bit amazed at how calm Rachel was after that dumb question and stupid statement. Today, I'm exhausted just thinking about all the things that she accomplishes as a mom and a wife. I could never live a life of work–life fusion without her help. Who is helping you? Take a moment to appreciate that person…right now.

"How's that Working for the Family?"

Even though we've formed a pretty solid team, I still feel self-induced pressure to be at home more and at work more. Does this feel familiar? The good news is that I love to be at home and love to be at work. If you choose to spend more time on your career, your family might suffer. If you choose to spend more time with your family, your career might suffer. However, I've come to realize that this is my issue, not someone else's. The bottom line for me is that helping to lead my family is my most important task. **The success that we build within our home will make everything outside of our home more fulfilling.** Do what works for you and your loved ones.

To help me keep this at the top of my mind, I ask myself and my family, "How's that working for the family?" I learned that they have a different perspective. For example, when I'm gone, enjoying my chosen career path, I'm having a blast. Although by asking myself that question, I've learned that what's fun for me isn't necessarily fun for my family…mostly because I'm physically gone. The question, "How's that working for the family?" has helped us become closer by finding shared values. It has also helped us come to the understanding that, even with work–life fusion, there will always be some sacrifice to live our ideal lives.

"...Always Assess and Adjust Your Passions and Priorities."

Can you now see the bigger picture of how the three core fundamentals of APE(Attitude, Passions, Execution)come together to create the formula that will lead you to live a better, more successful, and happier life? My friend, Dee Dee Ugent, once said to me, **"Work–life fusion will get more difficult as your children grow and your parents age. Life is full of curveballs. The key is to remain flexible and always assess and adjust your passions and priorities."** I couldn't agree with her more. Change will happen. Don't ever stop being self-aware, as you continue to *Move to Grow*.

You Can't Check "Life" Off Your List

SHIFT your mentality from work–life balance to work–life fusion once and for all. **You don't clock in and out of life.** Your friends want you. Your coworkers want you. Your family wants you. Your passions want you. **Every minute is a chance to do something meaningful.** You really *can* live your life and execute what you love to do at the same time.

When you dance, don't dance into a corner. Instead, be the best dancer that you can be, and be sure to listen to the music while you enjoy the dance. Life is not a dress rehearsal. You cannot simply enjoy the prospect of arriving at the destination. Fulfill your ideal life right now and enjoy the journey...because you can't check "life" off your list.

Pay It Forward

Now that you're cruising in Gear Five and living the life you've always dreamed of living, it's time to pay it forward. In the next chapter, you'll learn how to inspire and impact other fellow travelers to *SHIFT* with you. Now is the time for you to pump the brakes, pick up some fellow travelers, and help others move from frustrated to fulfilled. Buckle up and hold on because your life, and the lives of many others, will never be the same.

"Fusion" Key Moves

- Define what work means to you.
- Strive to match your personal and work values.
- Be present and capture your most precious moments.
- Create your ID, the intersection of your values.
- Evaluate your work–life fusion with the following: Question of Passion and Move Matrix.
- Spend as much time as you can enjoying your values.

STOP Write down the *first thing* from this chapter's content that you will move to act on.

_____

_____

_____

_____

_____

SHIFT Roadmap: From Fusion to Impact

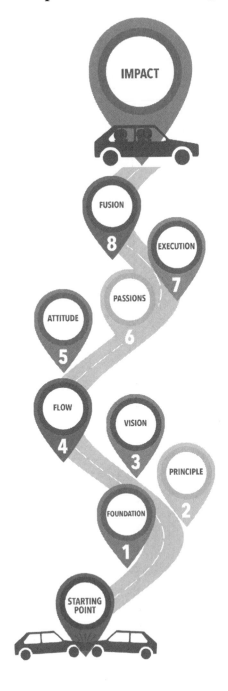

CONCLUSION

IMPACT:
INSPIRE FELLOW TRAVELERS

"Your life has purpose. Your story is important.
Your dreams count. Your voice matters.
You were born to make an impact."

– Unknown

O ne winter, my friend and former colleague, Margaret Offenbacher, asked me to coach her. Without hesitation, I said, "You bet!" because I knew the knowledge, skills, and ability she possessed. During our first session, Margaret kept saying, "There is something more inside me…something much, much bigger…I just need to get it out of me and do it." After listening to her say this over and over again, I finally responded to her by asking the question…"What are you putting off that's bothering you?"

> What are you putting off that's bothering you?

Margaret wrote down my question. After a couple of minutes, she asked, "Derek, could I have some extra time to really think about this? I'm not sure." "Definitely," I responded. "Self-reflective questions require some honest introspection."

The following week, Margaret sent me a message:

Derek, your question, 'What am I putting off that's bothering me?' has been incredibly thought-provoking! It really made me face what I have been avoiding (maybe dreading in a small way?), yet I KNOW once I address it…it will be life-changing. It asks me to leave my comfort zone and feel uncomfortable for a while, knowing it will be a lot of hard work. Like the feeling of jumping into a pool, I know I will be so happy I did, but those seconds of hesitation right before are so strong and powerful trying to keep me comfy and warm. This question is great because it will give me the push that I need to move forward.

Can you relate? Just think about the impact that one person and one question can make on someone.

For me, I forever left my comfort zone in 2008 when my mentor gifted me my first self-help book. Just look at how powerful her impact has been on me…

- In 2008, I was putting off personal development. Now, personal development is a part of my everyday life.
- In 2009, I was putting off becoming a better speaker. Today, I'm a professional speaker.
- In 2010, I was putting my family second, behind developing my career. I now try to blend my personal values at work and at home.
- In 2011, I was putting off stretching, but today I stretch twenty minutes per day.
- In 2012, I was putting off early wake-ups. Now, I wake up and get started at 5:00 a.m. every day.
- In 2013, I was putting off reading devotions, but now I read them almost daily.
- In 2014, I was putting off blogging weekly, but now I post a blog nearly every Wednesday.
- In 2015, I was putting off completing my book, but I finally signed with a coach and publisher, who guaranteed my book's completion.
- In 2016, I was putting off creating my ten-session Leadership Bootcamp, but I decided to complete one workshop per month until I was finished with the series.

Whenever I look back at my "I'd never do that" list, I think about Jim Rohn's quote, **"Whatever you move toward tends to move toward you."** As for Margaret, I'm overjoyed to report that she found her dream job one year later.

STOP **Put down your phone and grab a pen. Write down the** *one thing* **that you're putting off that is bothering you. Starting today, block off regular time in your calendar to get started on what's most important to you so that you will begin your journey. Let go of yesterday once and for all.**

One Thing: _____

"What One Word Best Describes You?"

Earlier in the book, I shared the best interview question that I was ever asked: "What is your plan for personal development?" While I bombed the answer, I made up for it later. During the same interview, I was asked a memorable final question: "What one word best describes you?" I paused and enthusiastically said, "Caring!" while I pounded my fist on the table and bounced my Vitamin Water cap to the ground.

Think about the one thing that you're putting off that's bothering you. Do you *care* about it enough to actually do it? More importantly, do you care enough about it to impact other peoples' lives for the better? If you don't care about where you're moving, you're not going to grow.

Dare to be Different

When you care enough about what you're doing, you just might impact someone so much that he or she will want to help you. As you know from my crash, I wanted to be a speaker. In August, 2013, I received an email from a mentor to schedule a coffee chat. When this person wants to meet, I do everything that I can to clear my schedule.

The day after, we met. We both ordered our coffees. Within seconds of sitting down, this person passed a greenish-blue card across the table. I said thank you and proceeded to place the card in my bag.

But this person said, "Go ahead...open it now." I said, "Oh, ok." I quickly read the front of the card, which said, "Dare to be Different." Then, I opened the card and read a personal message. Also inside was a loose sheet of paper which, to my surprise, was a generous gift! My jaw dropped.

Immediately, I said, "I can't take this." This person responded, "I'd be extremely disappointed if you didn't take it and go for it." With tears in my eyes, I whispered, "Wow."

"Just Pay It Forward."

This person recognized the fire that had been ignited in me and encouraged me to pursue my dream. This meant putting my APE concept into action to achieve a very specific goal. There was, however, one big caveat from this mentor..."Just pay it forward."

Long story short, I went on to become a John Maxwell Team (JMT) certified leadership speaker, facilitator, and coach. And it should come as no surprise to you that "paying it forward" turns out to be highly rewarding and impactful for everyone involved.

The lesson: fulfillment is about helping others, too. It doesn't have to be a big gift...it could be a quote, time, a book, or something else that would inspire that particular individual.

"It Doesn't Matter If They Apply It or Not."

Six months after I received the life-changing gift, I was officially speaking nationally. I'll never forget the time when someone stopped by my office and said, "Speaking sounds awesome. You get to fly in, speak, fly out, and it doesn't matter if they apply it or not." Inside, I was angry, but calmly responded, "My goal is for my presentations to have grandchildren...better yet, great-grandchildren. I teach what I love to the audience, and then I want them to share their favorite points with someone else." **To make an impact, you must care about others and love what you do.**

My mentor gave me the nudge that I needed to get out of my comfort zone because this person knew that I'd go for it and apply what I'd learned. I didn't do it by myself. Someone genuinely believed in me and wanted to help me. Whenever I think of this person, I think about this quote by former president John Quincy Adams, **"If your actions inspire others to dream more, learn more, do more, and become more, you are a leader."**

STOP Who Will You Help to *SHIFT* and Move from Frustrated to Fulfilled?

Imagine your story of fulfillment not ending with you, but starting with you. Just like my goal is for my keynotes and workshops to have great-grandchildren, my goal for this book is to have the same impact. I believe that we all want to help and inspire others, so my hope is for you to pay it forward. Take a moment and write down the name of one person that you want to help *SHIFT* and move from frustrated to fulfilled.

Person you will help: _____

Now that you know who you'll help to *SHIFT*, what knowledge or resource will you share with him or her?

Resource you will share: _____

"You Look Like You Don't Care."

On a Sunday afternoon in the middle of winter, my family and I were in the art studio at Discovery World, a science and technology center in Milwaukee, Wisconsin. Rachel was helping Ellie with a project. I, on the other hand, zoned out. Rachel said to me, "Derek, you look like you don't care."

I shook my head in embarrassment and responded, "I don't know why I'm not focused." Rachel replied, "I know why. You don't love art, but Ellie does. Think about your book. You love that, so you stay focused." For the rest of the day, I felt selfish… and rightfully so.

I wish I could go back to that day at Discovery World, but I can't. Instead, I will learn and make an impact next time. Moving forward, I will be engaged with Ellie's art projects because *she* loves them and because I care about *her* growth and development.

"Turn Your Passion into Compassion."

Fast forward a few months…we had our annual employee party at the athletic club. This year was extra special because we were celebrating our fortieth anniversary by launching our first Hall of Fame class. One of the inaugural members was health and fitness industry pioneer Sandy Coffman.

Sandy said something in her speech that I'll never forget: "When you turn your passion into compassion, you'll make a difference in their lives, but they'll also make a difference in your life." Sandy's compassion inspired all 500 people in the audience. Passion is about "you" and compassion is about the heartfelt connection between "them" and "you." Compassion is your desire to help someone. If you truly love something or someone, you'll positively impact them. Then, the positive impact on them will make you feel like you've made a difference in the universe.

> When you turn your passion into compassion, you'll make a difference in their lives, but they'll also make a difference in your life.

How Do You Create a Line Out the Door at 4:45 a.m.?

It was a late Sunday morning, and I was on my way to the gym to attend a going-away event for my friend and former colleague

Bethany Heinzerling. Bethany wanted to celebrate her move from Wisconsin to New York with a cycle class for her friends and coworkers. Since she wanted a high-energy class, Bethany asked Shahab Rahman, also known as Dr. Spin, to take the lead.

Throughout the farewell class, I wore my heart rate monitor and was in the red zone, which is 90 percent of my maximum heart rate, for most of the class. While I don't recommend that, I couldn't help it…there was just so much energy in the room. I kept thinking to myself, "How does Dr. Spin regularly create a line out the door at 4:45 a.m., even in the middle of winter, for his 5:00 a.m. cycle classes? He's not the most technical instructor."

In no time, I got my answer—compassion. The night before, Dr. Spin created a Pitbull playlist per Bethany's special request. He arrived an hour early to set up the room and engage in conversation by first name with all the cyclers. Dr. Spin did a countdown, 10–9–8…3–2–1, and yelled, "Showtime!" to launch the class. He delivered with passion and a positive attitude for all forty-five minutes. Dr. Spin even stayed to answer questions until the last person left.

If I Didn't Show Up, Would Anyone Miss Me?

During the cool down, I couldn't shut my mind off. I thought, "What if Dr. Spin hadn't shown up today?" We would've been so disappointed. Then I thought about my day job…"If I didn't show up, would anyone miss me?" I hope so.

How can you move others to join what you care deeply about? Dr. Spin creates waves because he sees opportunities and runs with them. **Movement of the masses can start with one person, but only when you care enough about pouring into the lives of others.** A standing ovation starts with one…and Dr. Spin earned one that day. To move others toward growth, it starts with one. Will it be you?

The Key to Moving Is *You*

I talk to many business leaders who try to get their employees hooked on personal growth; however, most of them are still waiting for their employees to take action. Throughout this book, you've learned how to grow. Don't be like "those people" and fail to execute. Be the person who takes the leap! **Personal growth starts with one person...*you*.** You only need a moment of your 1,440 minutes per day to make the decision to *SHIFT*.

STOP **Think about what you've learned in this book. You're the driver. What's the most important next step to help you carry out your vision?**

_____

_____

_____

_____

_____

The Moment My Influence Exceeded My Position

It was a typical Wednesday morning and I had just posted on my blog. The title was "Eat the Banana, Not the Frog." When I arrived at my day job a few hours later, there were a few bananas on my desk. Within an hour, outside my office, there was a short line of people who wanted to talk about the article. That afternoon, while I was in the locker room, a member said, "Nice article. You have no idea how many people read your posts." I had tons of email responses thanking me for the post. The next night, I had an event for the National Speakers Association and a few people referred to me as the "Banana Guy" that evening.

I'm never satisfied with myself, but when people say or write that I've made a positive difference in their lives, I'm satisfied for a moment. Stay the course. Your influence will exceed your position, too.

"Why Do You Share?"

When I played basketball in high school, I loved to score as many points as I possibly could. When I didn't score my average, people would talk. My coach, Reverend Tim Lindloff, said that I had to assist or share the ball more with others if we wanted to win conference and go to the state tournament. Coach Lindloff was right. When I stopped worrying about what other people thought, and I started thinking about how to impact others, we won conference and went to the state tournament.

One day at the gym, someone asked me, "Why do you share all of your secrets?" I replied, "I share everything because I love sharing new ideas, and it forces me to continue to learn and grow." The impact is a win–win. There is always something for them to gain, and there is always something for me to learn.

This directly applies to you when you apply the *Move to Grow* principle. You win by growing, and the people around you win by feeding off your attitude, passion, and execution. When the people around you grow, that is when the multiplication begins.

"Isn't It Easy?"

Throughout the book, you probably didn't learn anything too complex or unreachable. In fact, you've probably been like a bobble-head nodding at how this all makes sense. Since I've started to teach people about growth, I'm amazed at how many people email or stop by, and say, "Derek, I'm confused as to why this growth thing is so hard for people. Isn't it easy?" If personal growth was easy, more people would invest in it. It's not easy. You do, however, possess everything that you need to maneuver any roadblock, detour, or obstacle that you encounter along your journey. *SHIFT* is your lifelong roadmap to keep you committed. **You have to choose something...why not personal growth?**

A Way vs. the Way

If you've read this far, congratulations! You've already made the choice to *SHIFT* and grow. Your life will never be the same. Because personal growth is *personal*, I simply showed you a way to grow, not "the way." Unlike most books, there is a different ending for every person who reads *SHIFT*. **I'm inviting you to create your own ending.** To me, success is living your ideal day right now. What does success mean to you?

Our Journey Together

Let's briefly recap our journey together...

In "Crash," you learned that confronting and sharing your deepest fears and failures can start an incredible journey. I didn't start moving, growing, and impacting others until I realized the frustrations that I was hiding from others is what they wanted to see. Be open and honest with yourself and others. How will you forever crush your crash?

In "Foundation," you learned that to have a better chance at living your ideal life, you had to slow down in order to speed up, by writing down your personal core values. How will you make your values a part of your intentional daily living?

In "Principle," you were encouraged that it's never too late to grow by embracing the *Move to Grow* principle. You learned that it's important to connect the cues from your past, present, and future by moving, adjusting, moving more, and adjusting more. How will you have fun growing and following the cues that get you excited?

In "Vision," you learned that knowing your preferred future is your motivation for the choices that you'll ultimately make during your journey. Your vision touches your heart, and can turn a "have to" process into a "want to" flow. How will you move in the direction that you are being led?

In "Flow," you learned the three things that you have the power to control: Attitude, Passions, and Execution. The long-term discipline of APE precedes growth. Be patient. How will you appreciate the messy journey toward fulfillment?

In "Attitude," you learned that when you are positive, you create momentum toward your vision or preferred future. You can't truly *Move to Grow* or go anywhere in life without taking and accepting full responsibility for your attitude toward personal growth. How will you develop the will to be more positive?

In "Passions," you learned that when you align your life with your X, the intersection of what you love doing and what you want to be great at doing, you'll *Move to Grow* toward your ideal life. Don't die with your passions inside of you. How will you discover your X?

In "Execution," you learned that it's not the responsibility of other people to motivate and inspire you. Your values, vision, attitude, and passions should drive your behaviors for the rest of your life. How will you take action?

In "Fusion," you learned that by blending your values and passions in work and life, you can have a significant day and your quality of life improves. You created an ID that you actually like. How will you move from, "I need to be all things to all people," to, "I'm laser-focused on living my ideal life right now?"

In "Impact," you learned that when you turn your passion into compassion, you'll create a line outside your door and inspire others to grow. You measure your growth through your impact. How will you contribute to the success of others and pay it forward?

The High Occupancy Vehicle (HOV) Lane

Are you ever frustrated because you are stuck in traffic alone? In the 1970s, the United States slowly adopted High Occupancy Vehicle (HOV) lanes to help increase the number of people in each vehicle, with the goal of decreasing road congestion. In other words, traveling is better with a partner.

My Fellow Traveler

I'm going to grow until I die. You're going to grow until you die. But now that we're partners, we're going to grow together. Fellow traveler, you'll move mountains. I'll be here when you need me. Just promise me one thing…that you'll help at least one other person to grow and *SHIFT*, too. **When you bring out the best in yourself, you can bring out the best in others. Move you, move others.**

Your Fellow Travelers

It's my humble privilege that two of my fellow travelers, Ellie and Mia, are sitting in the backseat of my car on the way to school every morning. Little do they know that I tilt my rearview mirror down just enough so that I can cherish every second of their growth. Are your fellow travelers right behind you? Don't look too far.

Your Moves Will Last a Lifetime

Now, go on. *SHIFT! Move from frustrated to fulfilled.* Today marks the first day of the rest of your life, your journey, your awakening. I can't wait to see what's next. When an obstacle gets in the way of you and your ideal life, move it. Your moves will last a lifetime and will be the legacy that you've always dreamed of leaving. The drive continues…What's your next move?

> Your moves will last a lifetime and will be the legacy that you've always dreamed of leaving.

"Impact" Key Moves

- Dare to be different.

- Stop putting off the significant things you're not doing that are bothering you.

- Pay it forward by helping someone else *SHIFT*.

- Write down the critical next step to help you carry out your vision.

- Move the obstacle that is standing in the way between you and your ideal life.

STOP **Write down the *first thing* from this book's content that you will move to act on.**

_____

_____

_____

_____

_____

HOW TO MAKE A *SHIFT*

Introduction – CRASH: Confront Your Deepest Frustrations

Confronting and sharing your deepest fears and failures can start an incredible journey. You'll start moving, growing, and impacting others when you realize the frustrations that you are hiding from others is what they want to see. Be open and honest with yourself and others. How will you forever crush your crash?

Gear One – FOUNDATION: Form Your Core Values

To have a better chance at living your ideal life, slow down in order to speed up, by writing down your personal core values. How will you make your values a part of your intentional daily living?

Gear Two – PRINCIPLE: Pursue Personal Growth

Be encouraged that it's never too late to grow by embracing the Move to Grow principle. It's important to connect the cues from your past, present, and future by moving, adjusting, moving more, and adjusting more. How will you have fun growing and following the cues that get you excited?

Gear Three – VISION: Visualize Your Preferred Future

Knowing your preferred future is your motivation for the choices that you'll ultimately make during your journey. Your vision touches your heart, and can turn a "have to" process into a "want to" flow. How will you move in the direction that you are being led?

Gear Four – FLOW: Follow the APE Formula

There are three things that you have the power to control: Attitude, Passions, and Execution. The long-term discipline of APE precedes growth. Be patient. How will you appreciate the messy journey toward fulfillment?

ATTITUDE: Adopt a Positive Mindset

When you are positive, you create momentum toward your vision or preferred future. You can't truly Move to Grow or go anywhere in life without taking and accepting full responsibility for your attitude toward personal growth. How will you develop the will to be more positive?

PASSIONS: Personalize Your Ambitions

When you align your life with your X, the intersection of what you love doing and what you want to be great at doing, you'll Move to Grow toward your ideal life. Don't die with your passions inside of you. How will you discover your X?

EXECUTION: Exercise Meaningful Action

It's not the responsibility of other people to motivate and inspire you. Your values, vision, attitude, and passions should drive your behaviors for the rest of your life. How will you take action?

Gear Five – FUSION: Fulfill Your Ideal Life

By blending your values and passions in work and life, you can have a significant day and your quality of life improves. You'll create an ID that you actually like. How will you move from, "I need to be all things to all people," to, "I'm laser-focused on living my ideal life right now?"

Conclusion – IMPACT: Inspire Fellow Travelers

When you turn your passion into compassion, you'll create a line outside your door and inspire others to grow. You measure your growth through your impact. How will you contribute to the success of others and pay it forward?

To receive this complimentary resource, please visit DerekDeprey.com/ShiftBookResources

ACKNOWLEDGMENTS

To **Rachel Deprey**, my wife, best friend, biggest fan, and honest soundboard—thank you for your love, patience, and encouragement throughout this journey. You always give me the freedom to grow. Without you, I'd still be trying to become a professional basketball player. Your support of this book has been unwavering, and you've been my voice of reason throughout the many twists and turns. You believed in *SHIFT* when it was just a dream. I love you.

To **Kary Oberbrunner**, my friend and coach—thank you for believing in this first-time author. Thank you for being in the trenches and working side-by-side with me. *SHIFT* would not be what it is without you.

To **Mary Ziegler**, my mother-in-law and wordsmith—thank you for contributing greatly to the development of content and for your remarkable talents in helping me to edit this book. Your contributions raised *SHIFT* to a whole different level.

To my advanced readers and editors—thank you for making this book even better.

Abram Anderson, Mike Bartel, Paul Becker, Jeremy Bock, Sara Brugman, Calman Hilkert, John Johnson, Cami Karnthaler, Madelyn Kempen, Mike Kinsella, Sarah Knot, Kevin Koehler, Deanne Lachner, Precyl Larkins, Randy Leiberg, Jason Lowrey, Kevin Martinez, Rainer Meisterjahn, Chez Misko, Keith Nygren, Ray O'Connor, Deb Orr, Andrew Powers, Greg Schmill, Dee Dee Ugent, Megan Westra, and Nikki Wille

To all my family members, friends, mentors, and colleagues—thank you for pouring so much of your knowledge and experience into my life. There is a part of each and every one of you in this book.

To all my fellow travelers who are subscribers to **DerekDeprey.com**—thank you for your ongoing loyalty.

ABOUT THE AUTHOR

First and foremost, Derek is a husband to his beautiful wife, Rachel, and a proud father. He's been blessed with two curious and energetic daughters, Ellie and Mia, who constantly remind him of the simple joys in life.

Much of Derek's day is spent as the director of training and development as well as a general manager for the Wisconsin Athletic Club (WAC), where he teaches his staff the core principles of leadership, training, and personal development.

Shortly after joining the WAC, Derek couldn't get enough of what he was studying, learning, and applying, so much that he created his own business, Move Results, as an avenue to engage and impact others through motivational speaking, leadership skill-building facilitation, coaching, and writing. He is the author of *SHIFT: Move from Frustrated to Fulfilled*. Derek feels that the best business to start is one that you need yourself. He just knew it was right because, still to this day, he goes to bed and wakes up every morning excited to pursue his business. It truly blends his day job and dream job.

Derek's diverse career endeavors also include Wisconsin Lutheran College as an adjunct professor of adult and graduate studies. Additionally, he is certified to teach content from John Maxwell, Franklin Covey, and Ken Blanchard.

In his past career, Derek spent four years as a video scout in the NBA with the Milwaukee Bucks, two years as the coordinator of basketball operations in the NCAA with Marquette University, and one year as the director of player development with the University of Utah.

If there's anything he's learned in the past decade, it's that now is the time to build your career, to shape your life, and to strategically work on laying the foundation for accomplishing your dreams and prospering to your true potential. While there are many people who try to accomplish this, very few of them are given a roadmap of where to start; thus, Derek hopes you will find him as your resource for getting your compass pointed in the right direction.

Connect at DerekDeprey.com

COULD ONE MOVE CHANGE YOUR LIFE?

Imagine author Derek Deprey personally coaching you through his transformational roadmap that allows you to journey through frustration and into fulfillment.

Imagine shifting from, "I'm so busy and stressed," to, "I'm living my ideal life right now."

Find passion and purpose through this powerful experience. You'll never look at yourself the same again.

Participants can join and have access to Derek from anywhere in the world.

Take your next step and join the Shifting Gears Team!

Move. Grow. Achieve.

To find out more, please visit:
DerekDeprey.com/ShiftingGearsTeam

BRING DEREK INTO YOUR
BUSINESS OR ORGANIZATION

5 Reasons to Hire Derek as a Speaker or Facilitator

1. Derek is **PASSIONATE**…he brings the highest possible level of energy and enthusiasm.
2. Derek is **VULNERABLE**…he shares his failures and teaches you how to learn from them.
3. Derek is **PREPARED**…he pre-surveys your team and studies your business or organization.
4. Derek **CUSTOMIZES**…he integrates your mission, vision, values, goals, and pre-survey feedback.
5. Derek **INSPIRES**…he motivates your audience to act long after your event and creates a tailored handout with action items.

For Topics, Please Visit:

- **DerekDeprey.com/Speaker**
- **DerekDeprey.com/Facilitator**

"Derek has an infectious presence! He is on fire for contributing to the effectiveness and fulfillment of people. I've participated in Derek's professional development sessions, and he has a great talent in front of a group. He is knowledgeable, encouraging, and a great teacher."

— *Aleta Norris, partner at Living as a Leader*

"Derek's tailored approach deeply engaged the audience and made for an enjoyable two-day event. We've already implemented a number of positive changes to our daily routines."

— *Shane Crawford, city manager at Madeira Beach, Florida*

"Derek really hit the nail on the head with his full integration of our company values. The number of interactive exercises with genuine thinking for our team was perfect. The office is now buzzing with energy!"

— *Cindy Abraham, GE Capital*

**CONTACT DEREK TODAY TO
BEGIN THE CONVERSATION
DerekDeprey.com**

Made in the USA
Lexington, KY
20 September 2017